W9-BAW-897

MODERN DRAMATISTS

Modern Dramatists

Series Editors: Bruce and Adele King

Published titles

Further titles in preparation

MODERN DRAMATISTS

HAUPTMANN, WEDEKIND AND SCHNITZLER

Peter Skrine

St. Martin's Press   New York

First published in the United States of America in 1989

Printed in the People's Republic of China
ISBN 0-312-02676-5

Library of Congress Cataloguing-in-Publication Data

Skrine, Peter N.
     Hauptmann, Wedekind and Schnitzler / Peter Skrine.
       p. cm.—(Modern dramatists)
     ISBN 0-312-02676-5: $36.00 (est.)
     1. German drama—20th century—History and criticism.
   2. Hauptmann, Gerhart, 1862-1946—Criticism and interpretation.
   3. Wedekind, Frank, 1874-1918—Criticism and interpretation.
   4. Schnitzler, Arthur, 1862-1931—Criticism and interpretation.
     I. Title.   II. Series.
     PT667.S57 1988
     832'.8'09—dc19   88-23956
                                                                 CIP

For Celia

Contents

vii

Contents

List of Plates

1. Gerhart Hauptmann, c. 1895; Frank Wedekind, c. 1905; Arthur Schnitzler, c. 1910.
2. Gerhart Hauptmann, *Rose Bernd*, (Nationaltheater, Mannheim, 1984). Photograph: Hans-Jörg Michel.
3. Gerhart Hauptmann, *Rose Bernd* (Nationaltheater, Mannheim, 1984). Photograph: Hans-Jörg Michel.
4. Frank Wedekind, *Lulu* (Komödie, Basle, 1985). Photograph: Peter Schnetz.
5. Frank Wedekind, *Der Marquis von Keith* (Burgtheater, Vienna, 1982). Photograph: Elisabeth Hausmann.
6. Arthur Schnitzler, *Liebelei*, in Tom Stoppard's adaptation *Dalliance* (National Theatre, London, 1986). Photograph: Zoë Dominic.
7. Arthur Schnitzler, *Reigen* (*The Round Dance*) (Akademietheater, Vienna, 1983). Photograph: Victor Mory.
8. Arthur Schnitzler, *Reigen* (*The Round Dance*) (Komödie, Basle, 1981). Photograph: Peter Schnetz.

The author and publishers are grateful to the theatres and photographers named above for kind permission to reproduce plates. Many German, Austrian, Swiss and British theatres were kind enough to place programmes and other illustrative material at the author's disposal. Their readiness to help has been much appreciated.

Editors' Preface

The *Macmillan Modern Dramatists* is an international series of introductions to major and significant nineteenth- and twentieth-century dramatists, movements and new forms of drama in Europe, Great Britain, America and new nations such as Nigeria and Trinidad. Besides new studies of great and influential dramatists of the past, the series includes volumes on contemporary authors, recent trends in the theatre and on many dramatists, such as writers of farce, who have created theatre 'classics' while being neglected by literary criticism. The volumes in the series devoted to individual dramatists include a biography, a survey of the plays, and detailed analysis of the most significant plays, along with discussion, where relevant, of the political, social, historical and theatrical context. The authors of the volumes, who are involved with theatre as playwrights, directors, actors, teachers and critics, are concerned with the plays as theatre and discuss such matters as performance, character interpretation and staging, along with themes and contexts.

BRUCE KING
ADELE KING

A Note on Translations

All the translations in this book are my own. The titles of the plays are given in English translation to help the reader with no knowledge of German: their German titles are supplied in brackets at the first mention. An English title does not necessarily imply that the play in question exists in an English translation or has ever been performed in an English-language version. See the Note on Performances and the section on 'The Plays in Translation'.

P.S.

General Introduction

When we in the English-speaking countries think of drama around 1900, the plays that most readily come to mind will probably be by Chekhov and Shaw or, in lighter vein, by Oscar Wilde or Feydeau. The works of these authors, and of Ibsen before them, colour our view of the period. In our mind's eye we see ladies in white under white parasols conducting endless, clever dialogues with idealistic young intellectuals or elderly men of the world in summer gardens or on the white-painted terraces of houses in the country; or we remember equally fluent but rather more witty conversations over teacups and cucumber sandwiches in Edwardian drawing-rooms, and astute gentlemen and archly pretty women passing in review the problems of the world they lived in, the trivial shot through with graver implications. This, at least, is the impression generally conveyed by the plays which have survived from the turn of the century. But how accurate is this impression, and what does it leave out?

Around 1900 the German-speaking countries produced three outstanding dramatists: Gerhart Hauptmann (1862–1946), Arthur Schnitzler (1862–1931) and Frank Wedekind

1

(1864–1918). Yet outside these countries it is often not realised that at the turn of the century the theatre in both Germany and Austria was rich in talent and alive with exciting new ideas. Theatrically speaking it was a golden age. This was due to a combination of circumstances, of which the most immediately influential was the convergence in Berlin, and to a lesser degree in Vienna, of a number of enterprising theatrical managers, imaginative producers and gifted playwrights who were eager to put over their new conception of drama and ready to take the risk of confronting the public with the shock of the unexpected. A factor which helped them to achieve these goals was the backing they received from critics and reviewers in the quality press. Even a hostile notice could help, because it brought publicity and aroused interest at a time when theatre-going was still a favourite pastime of educated people, who enjoyed discussing the qualities and defects of the plays they had just seen or read. Book publication played a much more influential part in the propagation of new ideas, even in drama, than is often realised nowadays, and German audiences were particularly noted for their readiness to do their homework before attending a live performance.

The tendency to take theatre seriously has been an important factor in German theatrical history ever since the eighteenth-century critic and playwright Lessing was invited to become the resident critic of the Hamburg National Theatre in 1767. Schiller's famous essay 'The Stage Viewed as a Moral Institution' (written in 1784) gave authoritative voice to a view still in evidence in the German-speaking countries today: that the theatre has an essential social or political function and should be seen to uphold morality, speak the truth, and encourage audiences and their legislators to think, and to adapt to new ideas. German audiences are happy to accept that entertainment can be combined with serious aesthetic pleasure and an intellectual challenge; indeed, this has been a characteristic of the spoken theatre in German ever since the classical age of Lessing, Goethe and Schiller, whose plays provided the core of the serious repertoire. The picture this conjures up may be one of Teutonic seriousness, but it should also be noted that this earnestness is frequently offset by the readiness of German producers and companies to experiment with new techniques in stagecraft. Otto Brahm, Max Reinhardt, Erwin Piscator and Peter Stein provide outstanding examples.

By the middle of the nineteenth century almost every German-speaking town and city boasted its own theatre, and theatre-going was firmly established amongst the broad mass of the growing urban population. Between 1870 and 1896 the number of theatres actually trebled. Yet amongst the playwrights themselves there was a dearth of original talent. The momentum had gone out of the creative German dramatic tradition. The breakthrough of a new golden age in German drama came in 1889 in Berlin. In 1871 the city had become the capital of the new German Empire, and it was fast becoming the leading cultural centre of German-speaking Europe. Inspired by the social dramas of the Norwegian writer Ibsen (1828–1906), who spent much of his time in Germany, Gerhart Hauptmann provided the German stage with a series of great plays written between 1889 and 1911, which in Germany were, and still are, regarded as a continuation and fulfilment of the trend inaugurated by *The Pillars of Society* (1877), *A Doll's House* (1879), known in Germany as *Nora*, and *Ghosts* (1881). Hauptmann's realistic social dramas were stark, uncompromising portrayals of contemporary reality and of the problems confronting modern people within the sometimes bewilderingly complex social context of the new Germany. Alongside them, his main rival, Hermann Sudermann (1857–1928), provided the Berlin public with effective, well-made social plays such as *Heimat* (1893), which became better known outside Germany as *Magda*. The play is a classic of the

1890s, and it put German drama back on the map all over the world, and especially in the English-speaking countries. It was soon established as one of the most popular plays on the international circuit, thanks to its challenging title role of a spirited and independent girl who returns to her provincial home town as a world-famous singer, with disastrous results — a role which was relished by the great actresses of the time: Sarah Bernhardt, Eleonora Duse, Adele Sandrock, Olga Nethersole, Helen Modjeska, Minnie Maddern-Fiske and Mrs Patrick Campbell. Such recognition had never been accorded a German play before.

Around 1900 the German theatre was the equal of any in Europe. Why then is it so little known? None of the three dramatists to whom this book is devoted is now a household name in Britain or indeed in the United States, where there was at one time a readier response to their works — and to those of other German authors — thanks to the influential German element in the American theatre-going public. It is interesting to note that in 1897 the celebrated German actress Agnes Sorma (1866–1927) appeared at the Irving Place Theater in New York in works by Hauptmann and Schnitzler, and that, until 1917, most of Hauptmann's plays were given performances in German by resident companies in cities such as New York, St Louis and Milwaukee within months of their premières in Germany. Britain was less receptive. Though for a while Sudermann conquered the London stage (in 1895 both Duse and Bernhardt were to be seen there in productions of *Magda*, and Mrs Patrick Campbell followed suit in 1896), Hauptmann never achieved more than a toehold in Britain. As for Wedekind and Schnitzler, they were to benefit to some degree from the cultural revolution associated with the post-war permissive era: *Spring Awakening* was staged by the Royal Court Theatre in 1963 and productions of *The Round Dance* took place in Manchester and London in 1982, when the text came out of copyright. This, however, has tended to result in a lopsided view of these dramatists rather than in a level of acceptance in any way equivalent to that enjoyed by Chekhov and Ibsen in Britain or by a number of modern British authors in the German-speaking countries.

In spite of sporadic attempts, no producer or theatre company has really succeeded in acclimatising English-speaking audiences to the plays of Hauptmann, Schnitzler or Wedekind. Wedekind has perhaps fared best, and acquired something of the aura of an interesting oddity; but there is still a long way to go before he is generally accepted as one of the chief pioneers of modern theatre – a reputation he has long enjoyed in German-speaking countries. Schnitzler, for his part, has been helped to some degree of prominence thanks to the efforts of Tom Stoppard. His *Undiscovered Country* (1979) was a skilful adaptation of a great Austrian play, his *Dalliance* (1986) a theatrically effective distortion of another. As for Hauptmann, his total neglect is surely undeserved; it is time some enterprising theatre realised what theatrical experiences English-speaking audiences have been missing.

Can reasons be found for this neglect? One possibility is that German plays are assumed to be heavy and philosophical. With the curious exception of Brecht, they are regarded as too indigestible for an evening's entertainment – though the popularity of Wagner's music-dramas shows that German seriousness of artistic purpose can have wide appeal if presented in musical terms. Even Berg's opera *Lulu* is better known than the Wedekind plays on which it is based. Another reason may be the build-up of anti-German feeling since well before the turn of the century. This has made audiences instinctively hostile to plays set in German milieux, and producers are consequently reluctant to think of presenting dramas in which Germans figure as the embodiments of suffering, struggling, tragic yet often appealing humanity. The advantages Brecht enjoys in this respect are obvious enough: nowhere in the plays of his best known abroad – *Arturo Ui*, *The Caucasian Chalk Circle*, *The Life of Galileo* – are we asked to imagine ourselves in a typically or specifically German (or Austrian) setting. His plays stand before us as parables of human nature and conduct divorced from any specific German reality, though of course they are full of allusions to attitudes and events in Brecht's own country. Hauptmann and Schnitzler, and to a lesser extent Brecht's revered precursor Wedekind, adopt a very different approach. Their plays, or certainly their finest, are sensitive re-creations of time and place, of moods, attitudes, manners and behaviour observed as sharply and portrayed as sympathetically as Ibsen's Norway or Chekhov's Russia. The trouble is that, socially and culturally speaking, Germany and Austria are still undiscovered territory.

It is a vicious circle. Hauptmann and Wedekind could lead us into the German version of European society at the turn of the century if their plays were given the chance. But since we hardly ever get the opportunity to see these plays, that society remains for us far more alien than that of the small town on a Norwegian fjord or the datcha somewhere outside Moscow. Perhaps we feel that we know Vienna better, thanks mainly to operetta; but here too there are problems. One of the foremost is the relationship of Austria and its German-language literature to Germany as a whole. It comes as something of a surprise to discover that Schnitzler's reputation as the Viennese dramatist *par excellence* was made chiefly in Berlin, which responded to his evocation of the 'other' German city with greater enthusiasm than did his fellow-citizens, who tended to sense a note of satirical criticism underneath the Viennese charm and elegance which went down so well in the Prussian capital. A few words of explanation may be appropriate at this point to give readers enough background to understand and admire the achievement of the three great writers discussed in this book.

General Introduction

In 1889, when Hauptmann's first play inaugurated the new age in German drama, Germany had been a unified country like Britain for less than twenty years. Apart from Switzerland and the mini-states of Luxembourg and Liechtenstein, the only other independent German-speaking country in Europe was Austria. Officially, both states were relatively new. In 1867, after its defeat by Prussia in 1866, the Austrian Empire had been reorganised as a 'dual monarchy' called the Austro-Hungarian Empire; and in 1871, after Prussia and her German allies had also defeated France, a new German nation state, the Second Reich, had been created under the hegemony of Prussia, with the Prussian capital, Berlin, as its administrative centre. Yet the German-speaking portions of the Austro-Hungarian Empire had much in common with the German Empire ruled by Kaiser Wilhelm II: a language, a literature, a cultural heritage and a theatrical tradition which transcended the political frontiers recent history had imposed. For example the Vienna Burgtheater or Imperial Court Theatre was regarded as the arbiter of dramatic taste and elocution throughout the German-speaking world and was a focal point for its theatrical life: it moved into a splendid new building on the Ringstrasse in 1888. But the differences were perhaps greater than the similarities. The two German-speaking empires looked back on different historical traditions; their religious backgrounds were different (Austria exclusively Roman Catholic, the ethos of the German Empire predominantly Protestant), and economically, too, they were growing further apart as a result of Germany's massive industrialisation: in the period 1873–1914 Germany overtook Britain in productive capacity and turned from a mainly rural country into a manufacturing base second only to the United States.

If any one theme underlies the plays of Hauptmann and his fellow German Wedekind, it is that of change. Their plays, though vastly different in most other respects, are attempts to capture the feel of a society in a process of transformation; they focus on the problems and dilemmas faced by individuals as they try to adapt to change with more or less success. The Lulu plays, Wedekind's masterpiece, are a study in social mobility which charts a futile odyssey that ends up more or less where it began: on the streets. Hauptmann's *The Weavers* and *Before Sunrise* capture the multiple tensions brought about in communities and families by economic change on a scale which far transcends their limited powers of resistance or comprehension and which almost takes on the inevitable force and logic of tragic fate; against it even alcoholism or industrial strife prove to be no more than impotent gestures, since they may themselves be symptoms of the same process. The sense of change spreads upwards through society. Education brings dissatisfaction with background; the new scientific outlook provokes a break with the older generation, which in turn defends itself and its privileges by means fair and foul; tensions surface, gaps widen, conflict increases. Women take stock of their role in German society and in so doing call into question some of its most cherished notions; artists ask themselves what their vocation means: are they geniuses raised above the norm of humankind as the German Romantic and Classical traditions would both have it, or are they the servants of a basically philistine bourgeoisie which has the money to pay the piper and call the tune? Problems abounded wherever the dramatists looked, for, like many of the spectators who admired their new plays, they knew that something was rotten in the new nation state of Germany.

The result might have been a spate of wordy, indigestible problem-plays, had it not been for the fact that intellectual and sociological interests were matched, in Wedekind's case, by a natural flair for satire and the grotesque, and, in Hauptmann's, by an initially resolute adherence to the new creed of Naturalism – that concept of extreme, uncompromising realism which would brook nothing in literature or on the stage that was incompatible with the 'real life' being led by contemporary people wherever the author and his audience looked. The approaches of both playwrights precluded lengthy tirades and monologues, let alone asides to the audience. Instead, the audience had to be brought by subtler means to an awareness of the problems latent beneath a dramatic situation or dialogue and to a realisation that the author was concerned with more than just an evening's entertainment. The distinctive qualities of both playwrights naturally present considerable problems for the translator. Many a motivating factor or relevant background allusion gets lost when the text is divorced from its original social and linguistic context.

Not change itself but rather its illusory nature provides the underlying theme of Schnitzler's plays. Compared to Germany, Austria was backward-looking and set in its ways. Almost all Schnitzler's major plays are set in and around Vienna, a city which could look back on a glorious past and enjoy the sense of stability its long traditions created. In Schnitzler's world everything goes on much as it has always done, and, for the fortunate majority who can accept this in an easy-going way, life is remarkably pleasant. It is only on occasions, when someone senses the approach of dark mysterious forces and becomes aware that things may go wrong, that the comedy of life takes on intimations of tragedy. Thus the pleasant but monotonous life of Schnitzler's characteristic philanderers and men-about-town may sometimes be disturbed by unforeseen upsurges of passion or by the prospect of death in a duel fought for some relatively trivial reason. The irony is that the reason that rouses a person to adopt a serious attitude to life is in itself almost always trivial and not worth the trouble. And all the while the world goes on, indifferent to the fates of the insignificant men and women whose emotions Schnitzler analyses with as much skill and sensitivity as some of his Viennese contemporaries were bringing to their pioneering work in surgeries and psychiatric consulting rooms. For Austria, though it lacked Germany's new-found, dynamic sense of progress and purpose, was in its way contributing just as much to the emergence of the modern world.

Hauptmann, Wedekind and Schnitzler came from quite different parts of the pre-1914 German-speaking world. But they were exact contemporaries and it is not surprising that they were well aware of one another. As the most ebullient personality of the three, it was natural that Hauptmann should hold the central position among them. Schnitzler met him as early as 1896, when his own play *Free Game* (*Freiwild*) was given its Berlin première, and was delighted by his friendly attitude. They met again in 1902, when Hauptmann invited Schnitzler to visit him at his home in Silesia; another guest was Otto Brahm, the director of the Deutsches Theater in Berlin, a man to whose encouragement, courage and skill as a producer both authors owed very much.

Hauptmann had known Wedekind even longer; they first met in Zurich in 1888, when, it is said, they often discussed the extraordinary plays of Georg Büchner (1813-37), which were neglected in those days, but provided an enthusiastically admired model and starting-point for both playwrights. A rift ensued when Hauptmann made use of some confidential stories Wedekind had told him about his family background in his play *The Reconciliation* (*Das Friedensfest*). But he strove to make amends by putting in a good word for Wedekind's play *Pandora's Box* when it ran into difficulties with the censor, and expressed his admiration for *Spring Awakening*, in which Wedekind successfully tackled the problem of presenting children on stage, something that Hauptmann always avoided.

Schnitzler and Wedekind seem to have passed each other by, though they were aware of each other's work. Schnitzler saw Wedekind act the lead role in *Hidalla* in Vienna in 1907, and found the experience interesting from the technical point of view, though he expressed misgivings about the plays themselves apart from *Spring Awakening*, which made as deep an impression on him as it did on Hauptmann. In due course it became the custom in the theatre to couple Wedekind's one-act play *The Tenor* with one of Schnitzler's one-acters (such as *Literature* or one of the *Anatol* playlets): prior to 1920, however, Oscar Wilde's *Salomé* was preferred for this purpose, while Anouilh's *L'Orchestre* (1962) is now the conventional pairing.

The plays discussed in the following chapters represent their authors' most influential and lasting contributions to the modern theatre. Full coverage of their dramatic output is impossible in a volume of this size: Hauptmann wrote over forty full-length plays, Wedekind some twenty plays, and Schnitzler well over thirty, a good many of which are one-acters. In addition, all three, though best known as dramatists, published work in other genres. Hauptmann produced a large amount of interesting prose fiction, much of it based on his own experience, ranging from short stories in the Naturalist vein to an impressive account of religious mania in his native Silesia: *The Fool in Christ* (*Der Narr in Christo*), a novel published in 1910. Wedekind also wrote a number of narrative works, as well as some characteristically biting and ironic cabaret songs. Schnitzler, for his part, is perhaps better known nowadays for his masterly stories, among them *Lieutenant Gustl* (*Leutnant Gustl,* 1901) and *Fräulein Else* (1924).

A Note on Performances

The early stage performances of the major plays by Hauptmann, Wedekind and Schnitzler in Germany and Austria are now part of theatrical history. Since the Second World War, all three playwrights have continued to figure in the repertoire of the German-language theatre.* Hauptmann tops the bill and remains easily the most popular of the three with home audiences: that is, a small number of his plays have become staples of the German repertoire.

In the period 1947–75 thirty Hauptmann plays were given a total of 13,819 performances in the Federal Republic of Germany. *Der Biberpelz* (*The Beaver Coat*) and *Die Ratten* (*Rats*), his two great Berlin plays, continue to be far and away his most popular with the public, with *Fuhrmann Henschel* (*Drayman Henschel*) and *Rose Bernd*, two of his Silesian tragic dramas, coming some way behind.

The plays of Wedekind are not staged as often as they were before the Nazi period. Between 1947 and 1975 thirteen of his plays were produced, receiving a total of just 2185

* The performance statistics cited below were kindly provided by the Deutscher Bühnenverein.

performances. For a time the most frequently staged was his relatively uninteresting comedy *Der Liebestrank* (*The Love Potion*, 1900), though more recently *Frühlings Erwachen* (*Spring Awakening*) has returned to favour. Despite their reputation, the Lulu plays make only rare appearances in the theatre.

During the early part of the twentieth century, Schnitzler's plays vied with those of his two major contemporaries for the public's attention. His modern reputation in German-speaking theatres now centres on a relatively small number of plays, though in West Germany between 1947 and 1975 eighteen were staged, receiving a total of 1423 performances. *Anatol* and *Liebelei* are revived every now and then, as is *Der grüne Kakadu* (*The Green Cockatoo*); *Professor Bernhardi* has recently aroused renewed interest. Nevertheless the total of 340 performances achieved by *Anatol* in ten different productions (1947–75) hardly compares with *Der Liebestrank* with 713 in thirty-five productions, let alone with the 3995 performances achieved in 169 productions by *Der Biberpelz*. Nowadays, his popularity is understandably greater in Austria than in the Federal Republic or the GDR.

Outside the German-speaking countries the stage history of all three playwrights has been erratic. Before 1914 numerous attempts were made to introduce the dramas of Hauptmann to the British and American publics, but they have now lapsed into almost total neglect. Interest in Wedekind has remained sporadic in both the United States and Britain, where his reputation as an exponent of experimental theatre has recommended him to drama students but made him something of an acquired taste. Schnitzler's plays have always had their admirers, and one of them, *Reigen* (*The Round Dance*), reached a world-wide audience as *La Ronde* in the film version by Max Ophuls (1950), starring Danielle Darrieux and Gérard Philipe: the appealing Viennese-waltz theme was written by the veteran operetta composer Oscar Straus. In the English-speaking world Schnitzler has recently been making something of a comeback, thanks to *The Round Dance* and to Tom Stoppard's adaptations *Undiscovered Country* and *Dalliance*.

1
Gerhart Hauptmann

Hauptmann on Theatre

My ambition is to break new ground as regards dramatic technique. I want to free myself from the insistent claims of theatricality for its own sake, so as to get to something simple and totally true. In concentrating on theatrical effectiveness, many people lose sight of what is truly dramatic. True drama is found in human encounters and in the expression of relationships, in the movements of people in relation to each other as they meet, clash and circle round one another according to laws as natural as those governing the stars and planets. My starting-point must not be a preconceived formula put forward by others and not properly thought out; I must start out from my own experience, which for me is the only reality. This in all its complexity must be my basis, not artificially contrived plots, which are essentially false because they never happen in real life and cannot happen in plays if the characters are to remain consistent. Should today's men and women be excluded from drama just because they are unsuitable for plots of the traditional kind? No: today's drama must be provided by the

15

men and women of today, just as earlier drama was provided by the men and women of the past. Everyone is potential material for drama.   (Diary entry, 1906)

Wedekind on Hauptmann
What is lacking in everything I have written so far is the human warmth to which Hauptmann owes his powerful appeal.
(Letter, 1904)

Schnitzler on Hauptmann
Once again it is clear enough that of all the poets and playwrights at work in Germany or indeed in the world today, unquestionably the most gifted is Hauptmann.
(Diary entry, 1915)

Introduction

Gerhart Hauptmann's contribution to the modern theatre would be more obvious if his plays were better known outside the German-speaking countries. He was born in 1862 in a small spa town in Silesia, where his father was the proprietor of a hotel. From earliest childhood his surroundings made him aware of the different levels in society: on the one hand there were the locals, simple folk for the most part, who earned their living from weaving, mining and the tourist trade and spoke a Silesian dialect of German; on the other, there were the hotel guests, many of them titled people from Eastern Europe; and somewhere between came people like himself and his family, with roots in the hard-working weaving and farming communities of the area but with partially fulfilled aspirations to higher economic and social status. The stratification of society in general and the social mobility of individuals within it were to become central and complementary themes in his dramatic work; so, too, were the tensions he sensed between traditional attitudes and ways of life and the pull of the modern world, tensions which are often presented in his plays in terms of town and country or of the friction between the older generation and its successors.

At school Hauptmann showed little promise, and he explored a number of possible careers, from farming to sculpture, before finally deciding to take the risk of becoming a writer – a risk somewhat lessened by the financial support of the wealthy young woman who became his first wife. Following this decision, his perception soon broadened to include the predicament of the modern artist, a floater in the social spectrum, pulled this way and that by the demands of a largely middle-class reading and theatre-going public and by his own inner vision. Though rooted in provincial Silesia, its people and its countryside, he realised that his future lay in Berlin, which had become the cultural capital of a united Germany in 1871, and knew that he would never be a success as a playwright unless he succeeded in capturing the Berlin stage and gaining the support of its influential producers, actors and critics. Thanks to the backing of the critic and producer Otto Brahm, who was on the look-out for an exciting new writer, he established himself in Berlin from 1889, and soon became an authentic portrayer of life in the big city. Many of the basic tensions which we associate with the modern age found an early outlet in his plays.

Hauptmann was enormously productive. His creative imagination was vigorous and abundant, and, though his output of plays was large, it actually represents only a portion of what he wrote. Despite their great merits, his plays do not travel well. Attempts have been made to stage them abroad, but the failure of even the most famous ones to establish themselves outside the German-speaking world suggests that they do not form an integral part of our conception of modern drama. His rich contribution to the modern repertoire seems to have been

superseded or forgotten; even in the German-language theatre
his name now tends to be associated with a relatively small body
of works which actually represent only a fraction of his total
output. It is clear that his plays stand somewhat apart from the
central thrust of twentieth-century German drama, which points
from Büchner and Wedekind through to Brecht and Dürrenmatt.
Yet when Hauptmann is giving dramatic expression to the social
and psychological tensions of his period and questioning its
cherished assumptions and its self-image, his achievement is
unsurpassed. Indeed, it would be hard to find any European
or American playwright better able to bring the period from
1890 to 1940 to life in all its variety and with all its paradoxes
and contradictions. Theatrically, his art sums up an epoch.

If Hauptmann's appeal and reputation outside Germany are
nowadays slight compared to those of his close contemporaries
Chekhov (1860–1904), Shaw (1856–1950), and even
Schnitzler (1862–1931), this may well be mainly due to
ignorance of what Hauptmann's Germany was really like. Most
people have some idea of Habsburg Vienna and pre-
Revolutionary Russia, and their mental images owe much to
literature – indeed to playwrights such as Schnitzler and
Chekhov. These images may not be accurate, but they stand
producers and audiences in good stead. By comparison, most
people's picture of Germany, let alone of Silesia or even Berlin,
during the same period is hazy, if not non-existent. Such as it
is, it is often, in addition, distorted by attitudes and prejudices
going back to 1914, and by the notion that German culture is
high-brow, heavy and indigestible. As a result German plays
are in most cases regarded as inherently unsuited to the non-
German stage. They are only acceptable if they ridicule or
attack, and thus reinforce existing prejudices, or if they avoid
the particular German context in favour of other locations and
of more generalised themes. The success of Fritz Hochwälder's
The Strong are Lonely (*Das heilige Experiment*) and of Max

Frisch's *Andorra*, and of course the plays of Brecht, are cases in point. Yet nothing can bring Berlin or the countryside of Silesia and its small towns more vividly to life than a good Hauptmann play, well produced and well acted.

Paradoxically, the means whereby this is achieved are now his greatest liability as well as his greatest asset, for his plays do not depend primarily on subject matter, theme or even location: the stuff of his drama is language. His characters and the relationships between them, their often shifting social positions and their tragic insights, are all generated and communicated first and foremost in terms of language, which Hauptmann seems to catch and record as his characters are in the very act of speaking. At his best, he has no voice of his own; he seems merely to be the impartial recorder of what they happen to be saying. Being the sort of characters they are, they, too, are half the time unaware of its significance, and it is only when the dialogue is analysed more closely by producers, actors and readers that its complex patterns of underlying connections, rhythms and lines of thought emerge.

One might expect this sublime detachment to be Hauptmann's major asset as a playwright, but the fact is that he has had to pay a considerable price for it. During the last fifty years or so, styles of acting and production have changed, and linguistic registers and patterns of speech are in any case less easily co-ordinated than movement or lighting. Hauptmann now poses major difficulties even for German producers and audiences: the locations he favoured as settings for realistic plays are now all well outside the Federal Republic of Germany and have altered out of all recognition since he was writing. Admittedly Berlin is still a big city, but it is no longer central to the national consciousness – unlike London or Paris, which have retained their normative centrality both socially and linguistically. In Hauptmann's day Berlin was rejoicing in its new-found role as the political and cultural capital of Germany; now it has turned

19

into a symbol of international division. As for Hauptmann's Silesia, it has vanished off the face of the earth, taking with it not just a regional accent but a whole way of responding to life. (The region was absorbed into Poland after the Second World War.) This in turn has had a major impact on production techniques and performance figures: the contemporary German stage is finding it more and more difficult to cast the great Hauptmann plays and perform them with any hope of linguistic and socio-linguistic accuracy: hardly anyone in the German-speaking world of today can still speak with the Silesian regional accent required in nearly all Hauptmann's realistic plays. Instead producers have to make do with transcriptions into all-purpose contemporary German, an approach which may sometimes work but which tends to present an emasculated Hauptmann bereft of his most potent artistic medium.

Given the difficulties the plays present even for German-speakers, it is not surprising that it has proved difficult to translate them into other languages and to retain a sense of their extraordinary plausibility and vitality. Ludwig Lewisohn, Hauptmann's first major American translator, tells us in the Preface to volume 1 (1912) of the 'authorized edition' of Hauptmann's dramatic works in English that he found it necessary to 'invent a dialect near enough to the English of the common people to convince the reader or spectator, yet not so near to the usage of any class or locality as to interpose between him and Hauptmann's characters an alien atmosphere'. The translator's task remains the same today, especially as regards the social dramas of Hauptmann, which depend very much on linguistic differentiation and on the use of dialect for their effect. Perhaps the time is coming for Hauptmann to be approached from a different angle. It may be that through his other, less famous plays in standard German his enormous creative achievement can be won back for the international stage.

'Before Sunrise'

Hauptmann's first play is a good illustration of his qualities as a dramatist and of the difficulties with which he confronts modern audiences, especially outside Germany. It is seldom performed nowadays even there, yet it remains an astonishing achievement, powerful, disturbing, and deeply satisfying on a literary level. Hauptmann had provisionally moved to Berlin in 1884, and returned to settle there in 1888 after a stimulating six months in Zurich in the company of young intellectuals drawn from many parts of Europe. It was there, in the very different environment of the Swiss lakeside city, that the provincial German milieu in which he had grown up, and which he had left behind him to become a writer, rose up in his imagination in all its stark, crude intensity. The more he read and thought about the social problems back home, and the more he talked them over with people who were equally concerned about the state of contemporary society, the more clearly he realised the nature of the challenge facing him as a new dramatist. Gone were his grandiose dreams of poetic dramas on historical subjects. *Before Sunrise* (*Vor Sonnenaufgang*) is a savage exposure of the economic and social conditions prevailing in a provincial community woefully backward and hopelessly benighted despite the proudly optimistic claims of the contemporary exponents of progress. He calls the place Witzdorf, a name which may not appear in the gazetteer; but its location in a specific area of the Second Reich in the late 1880s was clear to all. What Hauptmann depicted in his play rang true.

In Berlin, Hauptmann had been learning a great deal. It was fast establishing itself as the main centre of the Naturalist movement in Germany, and the theorists and writers of the new movement stressed the central importance both in life and in art of environment and heredity, the factors which determine

21

what we are and what we do when it comes to the point. They also insisted on the artist's obligation to reproduce only what he can see before him, and to do so with as much accuracy and as much honesty as possible. From now on, human beings were no longer to be models for the artist's inspiration but objects of his detached and probing clinical observation. Environment or 'milieu' provided the descriptive, spatial element in the Naturalist conception of literature, the 'setting' of Naturalist dramas, while recognition of the influence of heredity called for the most meticulous attention to the family background of individual characters: in Naturalist writing characters can never be presented or understood in total isolation. What is decisive, however, is the moment in time. The Naturalists were convinced that what the human being does at any given moment is determined by his inherited physical and emotional make-up and the milieu in which he grew up or happens to find himself; what he does under the pressure of the moment must therefore be an immediate and accurate expression of his true nature. This had its corollaries for prose fiction and for the stage. What we see before us is what the characters are actually experiencing moment by moment as it unfolds into an uncertain future; and it unfolds against the background of the past although the setting is of course the present. Most Naturalist writers attempted to convey their artistic interpretations of these basic tenets in the form of novels and short stories. Hauptmann, however, saw their potential for a whole new conception of drama.

In *Before Sunrise* this new concept was realised overnight. All the basic elements of Naturalism – environment, heredity, and the pressures of the moment – are there at work, and Hauptmann uses them to generate a forward momentum which builds up dramatic suspense, thus overcoming the tendency of much ultra-realist writing to be static and descriptive. The secret of his success was an instinctive sense of stagecraft and of dramatic exposition. In traditional drama, exposition sets the scene for a dramatic conflict by putting the audience and the characters in the picture as regards the events which have led up to the 'ripe' situation prevailing as the curtain rises. In *Before Sunrise* Hauptmann extends exposition to include the whole duration and action of the drama; it is only fully complete when the dramatic action comes to an end. Moreover he had read and seen enough Ibsen to realise the wider potential of dramatic exposition for his purposes as a social dramatist. By making exposition almost synonymous with exposure, he fused his dramatic message with his medium. The protracted exposition which takes up virtually the whole of *Before Sunrise* amounts to an exposure of the ugly things that are going on behind a façade of prosperity and respectability. 'Indecent exposure', some people indignantly called it; even for some of the Naturalists it was almost too much. 'The stage is being turned into a dung-heap!' Hauptmann's colleague Conrad Alberti exclaimed.

What Hauptmann's first social drama revealed to the educated middle-class Berlin audience which first saw it in October 1889 was an uncomfortable truth: in the glorious new German Reich – unified, affluent, industrialised and powerful – appalling social evils were rife of which they were ignorant, or which they preferred to ignore. What the performance exposed to view was essentially topical and, as a result, it is now particularly interesting as a piece of social history. It dramatised the impact of industrial development on a rural community and how this resulted in a major change in living-standards, and in moral standards, too. The discovery of coal deposits underneath the fields and meadows of Witzdorf in Silesia has suddenly provided the local landowning farmers with a far richer source of income than agriculture could ever give them. Though in all probability they are being exploited in their grasping peasant gullibility by the mining company managed by Herr Hoffmann, the members of farmer Krause's family now have more than enough money to indulge in a life-style which they and their like had never dreamt of before. The situation is a familiar one: sudden economic change is always fraught with difficulties and dangers, and the ready availability of consumer goods and the veneer of higher living-standards can barely conceal the continued presence, beneath the surface, of ignorance, greed and misery. In the circumstances it is hardly surprising that the farmer and his family have taken to drink.

But how does one bring such a state of affairs to dramatic life? True to his Naturalist approach, Hauptmann sets the first act of his play in a location which speaks for itself: a low farmhouse room, in which modern luxury seems to have been grafted on to sparse peasant simplicity. To get the action moving, he adopts a technique which had already been perfected by Ibsen, whose *Ghosts* (1881) preceded the première of *Before Sunrise* during the same 1889 season of *avant-garde* plays staged in matinée performances at the Lessing-Theater, Berlin, by the Freie Bühne or 'Free Stage Society', an association formed to promote the Naturalist cause. In true Ibsen fashion, an outsider turns up soon after the curtain rises. His name is Alfred Loth (pronounced to rhyme with 'dote'), and his appearance and function are aptly and plausibly motivated: he is a recently qualified economist of working-class background, who is deeply concerned about the economic, social and moral state of the nation, and he has come to Witzdorf on a fact-finding mission to see new industry at work and ascertain what effects it is having. In order to gain first-hand information, he looks up Hoffmann, a former student associate of his who got a job in a mining company after graduating, and who is now doing well as an entrepreneur in Witzdorf, where his company has secured exclusive rights to mine coal. Hoffmann has married one of the daughters of a newly prosperous local farmer, but the marriage appears to be far from happy: one child has died in suspicious circumstances, and another pregnancy is proving almost too much for his debilitated wife. Understandably Hoffmann has his eye on Helene Krause, his wife's younger sister, an educated, sensitive girl fresh from boarding-school. And it is equally understandable that Helene should welcome the company of her brother-in-law's old university friend, with his fresh ideas and aura of the outer world, and see in him her saviour from a stifling situation in which she feels intellectually starved and sexually vulnerable. Loth, immature and immersed in his self-imposed altruistic mission, fails at first to appreciate the degradation and double standards of the Krause family, who make him so welcome, or the depth of feeling he arouses in Helene. We in the audience see more, however, than he does, with the result that we are already almost in the know while he is still finding out. When the stark truth dawns on him, it proves too much for this modern young hero with his advanced views; he is unable to accept the situation. Awakened to the fact that the people he has fallen amongst are depraved and benighted, he flees from their midst just as his namesake, Lot, fled from Sodom and Gomorrah. Being an enlightened young man, he is unable to face the social, moral and emotional implications of a state of affairs 'before sunrise'

Alcoholism is ostensibly the central concern of the play, right from the initial drink which Hoffmann offers and Loth refuses, to the final climax when Loth leaves Witzdorf and abandons Helene because she is incompatible with his fervently held views on eugenics and healthy marriage. Alcoholism was also one of the burning topics of the day; in Britain the temperance movement was at its height, while Germany's leading temperance organisation, the Blaues Kreuz (Blue Cross), was set up in 1892, three years after the première of the drama. During his stay in Zurich in 1888, Hauptmann had already made a first-hand study of the physical and psychological effects of alcoholism under the distinguished Swiss psychiatrist Auguste Forel and he was well aware that drinking and drunkenness were widespread as a result of a variety of identifiable social pressures: everywhere recognition was growing that many major social, moral and physical evils could be traced directly or indirectly to alcohol, and medical experts were becoming increasingly convinced that alcoholism was a hereditary disease. It was therefore an ideal subject for demonstrating the basic tenets of Naturalism in action (as Zola, the French novelist, had already done in his novel *L'Assommoir*, published in 1877), and it had the additional advantage of being an excellent theme for a social drama, since drinking activates a wide range of social behaviour. In Act I Hoffmann's welcoming glass is a social gesture intended to break the ice, while the orgy of gastronomic status symbolism to which we are treated in Act II, as dinner takes place on the Krause farm and oysters and lobster are washed down with champagne, illustrates the corrupting pleasures of new-found wealth. Loth disapproves of it all; his instinctive response is an impassioned defence of temperance in the midst of bibulous conviviality. Only later does he discover that the whole family, including Helene, is suffering from a condition for which there is no cure. To escape contamination he decides to cut and run, regardless of the consequences, leaving Helene to make an end of herself in solitary despair.

Hauptmann's first play is about much more than hereditary alcoholism amongst the *nouveau-riche* Silesian farming community. It is a drama concerned with human beings and their vulnerability to the pressure exerted upon them and from within them. One telling example is provided by the local doctor, Dr Schimmelpfennig, who in Act IV takes it upon himself to open Loth's eyes to the truth of the situation. His action seems altruistic enough; but are his words just the dispassionate advice of a conscientious physician, as we suppose and Loth assumes, or could they be prompted by deeper motivations? Are they a subconscious attempt (or even a deliberate one) to get rid of an interloper whose presence threatens to upset the *status quo* and has aroused the doctor's sexual jealousy? *Before Sunrise* is also about the desperate need of people for affection and admiration, and their bungled attempts to express their emotions and make a reality of their dreams and aspirations. In 1889 the love scene between Helene and Loth in Act IV caused shock waves. It now seems tame enough by comparison with Wedekind's Lulu plays or the explicit sexual encounters of Schnitzler's *Round Dance*, all of which were written within the next fifteen years; but this is a measure of the success of Hauptmann's first play in clearing the way for a revolution in attitudes (accomplished far earlier in Germany than in Britain) towards the frank treatment of sexual matters on stage. The freedom with which Helene breaks through social convention and her own inhibitions by offering Loth her love struck contemporaries as brazen in the extreme; we are more likely to be horrified by the incestuous advances made towards her by her drunken father as he reels home from the pub, or by the terror that she confesses to Loth she feels each time she encounters the staring eyes in the coal-blackened faces of the miners as they trudge past her home on their way from the pithead. The essence of Zola's epic treatment of the tensions in a coal-mining community in his famous Naturalist novel *Germinal* (1885) is caught in a fleeting moment. Helene spoke for millions.

Ibsen called *Before Sunrise* bold and courageous. It was certainly bold to take a typical representative of the 'new' human being – scientifically educated and sociologically aware – and make him the agent of a tragic exposure of a sick society, and from the aesthetic and dramatic point of view it was equally courageous to present the public with a demonstration of the Naturalist approach which shunned all compromise with the 'well-made' type of play the public loved, a compromise adopted with great success by Hauptmann's first and only major German rival, Hermann Sudermann (1857–1928), whose first play,

27

Honour (*Die Ehre*), was premièred by the Freie Bühne five weeks after *Before Sunrise* and appealed so much that it was taken up by 151 theatres in its first season. Hauptmann's play was not such a box-office success, though its uncompromising approach was to make its fame more lasting. In it, sociologically significant detail is given maximum attention, much of it in the form of meticulous stage-directions. This was a characteristic device of Naturalist dramatists and was soon taken up by Shaw; indeed it is evident in some earlier plays such as T. W. Robertson's social drama *Caste* (1867). Stage-directions of this detailed kind provided a challenge to producers and stage-managers, who were now called upon to achieve as high a degree of authenticity in contemporary drama as they were already proud of achieving in their productions of Shakespeare's and Schiller's history plays. It was also entirely in line with the artistic aims of Otto Brahm, chairman of the Freie Bühne. The stage-set specified for the room in the Krause farmhouse in Act I is a good example. Another change taking place in stage-production in the late nineteenth century is illustrated – or, rather, called for – as Act II opens. For the first few minutes the stage is empty; the setting is the Krause farmyard at 4 a.m. as dawn is breaking:

> There is light in the windows of the pub; pale grey morning light is creeping in through the farm gate. During the course of the action it turns into a deep red glow which then dissolves equally gradually into broad daylight.

These stage directions give a clear indication that Hauptmann's new type of realistic drama heralded a revolution in stage practice by inviting producers to make the most of the innovations in electric lighting being developed at the time and which managers were installing in many leading theatres in the later 1880s. Here at last was stage-lighting which could behave

28

as natural light does, making the varied effects of light and shade, of shapes, masses and movements, contribute their essential, vital quality to drama – as they do a few minutes into Act II, when the dark silhouette of Farmer Krause is seen stumbling to and fro as he makes his drunken way home from the pub. Sound-effects, too, take on a new dimension at this point in the play. At first the only audible sound is the monotonous noise of a farm implement being sharpened: this lasts several minutes, then is followed by total silence, broken in turn by the discordant sounds of late-night drinkers leaving the pub, bolts being drawn, the distant barking of a dog, and a cacophony of cock-crows. It could rightly be said that the countryside had been translated on to the stage and rendered almost palpable to the audience in aural and visual terms. From a technical point of view this was the play's most radical innovation.

Hauptmann provided another challenge too. He expected producers and actors to pay the closest attention to the speech patterns, linguistic registers and other telling features of his characters' language. *Before Sunrise* marked an end, for the time being, to the convention of classical stage diction which had played an important part in overcoming the linguistic and political fragmentation of the German-speaking world during the age of Goethe and Schiller. From now on, character, personality and social position were to be defined and conveyed in terms of language, and what mattered was not so much what people said as the way they said it. Helene's isolation, for instance, is intensified by the fact that her strict Protestant boarding-school education has taught her to speak 'correct' German, which is very far removed from the earthy dialect spoken by her father and audibly different from her stepmother's ludicrous attempts to 'speak above her station'. In her speech, Helene Krause is closer to the articulate, educated Loth and his former student associates, Hoffmann and Dr Schimmelpfennig, than she is to her own family, and this serves to reinforce her increasingly isolated position as well as making her love for Loth all the more plausible. One thing which Hauptmann knew right from the start of his career as a playwright was that the way people talk often says more about them than what they actually say or do. This insight was to be of paramount importance for modern drama.

'The Reconciliation'

Hauptmann's second play, *The Reconciliation (Das Friedensfest,* 1890), has never caught on, which is really rather strange. Although often treated as a minor work, it deserves close attention here because it is the direct creative response of one major German playwright to subject matter drawn from the real life of another. Wedekind had disclosed some intimate details about his home life to Hauptmann when they were both in Zurich in 1888, and when Hauptmann later worked them up into a play, Wedekind was not amused. This is not surprising, for the picture Hauptmann presents is not a flattering one. Its psychological authenticity, however, is corroborated by the fact that it also reflects the experiences of a great many other people, and it still rings uncomfortably true.

This time the location is the large entrance hall of a detached residence on the outskirts of Berlin; it is Christmas Eve, and, in keeping with the festive spirit, Frau Buchner, a well-meaning friend of the Scholz family, has done her best to bring its members together again. At first it seems that her efforts to effect this reconciliation will be rewarded. But the antlers and other hunting-trophies decorating the walls in German fashion, and temporarily trimmed with festive foliage, gaze ominously down on the proceedings: poor, hunted, cornered, slaughtered creatures, their presence casts long shadows over the cosy, pious

Christmas planned for the Scholz family. As its various members assemble, the action moves optimistically forward to the heart-warming moment when the Christmas tree is lit, coolness thaws and mutual reconciliations are all but complete. But what in fact takes place is a grotesque replay of all those countless occasions in the past when those present got on each other's nerves. Robert, the younger of the two Scholz sons and now aged twenty-eight, warns Frau Buchner in Act I what the outcome of her well-intentioned plan is likely to be:

> Quite honestly, your efforts are futile. None of this will come to anything. We are total wash-outs, all of us; our characters are flawed, and so was our upbringing as well. Nothing can be done about it. This all looks very pretty: the Christmas tree, the candles, the presents, the family reunion. But it's only superficial, and it's a pack of lies.

The truth of the situation as Robert sees it is a permanent state of mutual hostility made inevitable by the fundamental incompatibility of his now-estranged parents (modelled on Dr Wedekind and his wife, who like Frau Scholz was about twenty years younger than her husband). The children of this union – Augusta, Wilhelm and Robert – are also its victims, and are 'fated' to bear the almost intolerable physical and psychological burden transmitted to them by parents who should never have married each other in the first place. Robert, a likeable but cynical fellow closely modelled on Wedekind himself, accepts the Naturalist view that environment and heredity are determining forces, and later on in the play voices his opinion that there is no point in attempting anything which one is by nature incapable of achieving. Wilhelm, however, is ready to make this 'impossible' effort. Years ago, he had struck his domineering martinet of a father in the face after hearing him make disparaging remarks about his own wife, Wilhelm's

mother; now, the benign influence and moral support of Frau
Buchner and her daughter, Ida, have brought him to the point
at which it has become imperative for him to put the past behind
him and regain his self-respect by making amends and securing
his father's forgiveness. It is obvious that this is why Frau
Buchner has persuaded him to come back to the family home,
but whether the good lady was also responsible for the
unexpected return of Dr Scholz, and whether she has any inkling
that she is paving the way for an expiation of existential guilt,
is never made clear and is one of those mysteries which make
the play so convincing as a slice of real life.

The effort of will proves too much for Wilhelm. In Act II
the sound and sight of his father coming downstairs towards
him produces a state of violent agitation. In a tense sequence
during which not a single word is spoken, father and son
experience a replay of the emotional reactions which
characterised their relationship in the past. Wilhelm advances
towards his father; fear grips Dr Scholz that the whole scene
is about to be re-enacted; tension mounts, and the sequence
culminates as Wilhelm collapses unconscious at his father's feet,
prompting from Dr Scholz a spontaneous response of anxious
concern for his son. Yet, before many minutes are past, the
precarious truce is over, and they are at each other's throats
again, taken by surprise by a new turn of events which is at
once trivial and catastrophic. The Christmas presents Ida gives
the two brothers are not an unqualified success: Wilhelm is given
a purse which she had originally crocheted for her late father,
while Robert receives a new pipe as a replacement for his
favourite old one. Looking on, Dr Scholz drinks far more than
a man of nearly seventy should, especially when he has a severe
heart condition; and meanwhile the Christmas carol being sung
by some of the family in the next room, off stage, is so
hackneyed and seems to have so many verses. Wilhelm, growing
tenser by the minute, senses that his girlfriend Ida feels hurt

by the behaviour of his family; his nervousness erupts as he tells the carol-singers to shut up; the siblings quarrel; father, as usual, intervenes; tempers snap; and Wilhelm's efforts to pour oil on troubled waters have the opposite effect. When his hand happens to touch his father's arm, the latter's reflex action is symptomatic. Relapsing into the past under the pressure of the moment, he once again assumes that his own son is assaulting him. He relives his trauma, reacts violently, and collapses, felled by a massive stroke.

The climax of Act II makes engrossing theatre, and it brings Hauptmann into direct comparison with his main rival at the time, Hermann Sudermann, whose greatest success, *Heimat* (1893), known to the English-speaking world as *Magda*, makes use of a similar *coup-de-théâtre* to bring to an end a similar dramatisation of precarious reconciliation and ultimately triumphant antagonism between an authoritarian father and his prodigal offspring – in this case a daughter who ventured to leave home in order to go on the stage, and who has become a great actress. *The Reconciliation* could never hope to enjoy the international popularity that *Magda* achieved, and the reason why is simple: whereas Sudermann used life to create theatrical effects, Hauptmann created effective drama out of closely observed life. *Magda* met contemporary expectations half-way and provided challenges which the theatre of the period could meet; *The Reconciliation*, however, made unprecedented demands on producers, actors and audiences alike. Indeed, *The Reconciliation*, though written at the height of the Naturalist movement in Berlin, actually seems to transcend the limits of place and period and to point ahead to a concept of drama which was not to become familiar in Britain until Harold Pinter's *The Birthday Party* was first produced at the Arts Theatre, Cambridge, in 1958. Stylistically and technically it has more in common with Pinter's play than with the broad tradition of late-nineteenth-century realistic drama. This is seen for instance in the emphasis Hauptmann gives to movement and gesture, and to the repeated use of incomplete phrases which are sometimes almost incoherent: Frau Scholz's recurrent, mechanical 'Gottogottogott!' for example. The characters' words are often just one aspect of self-expression, and a relatively superficial one at that. As the central scene shows, dialogue in Hauptmann's realistic social dramas is often non-existent in the accepted meaning of the term. The words exchanged by his characters are often less important than their other, non-verbal gestures, their actions or indeed their silences. What interested him most at this point was not his characters' ability to articulate their deepest feelings so much as their innate inability to communicate. The bonds between them, either of love or hatred, operate at levels deeper and more subliminal than speech.

At the end of *The Reconciliation* Ida and Wilhelm are seen hand in hand entering the room, off stage, where Dr Scholz is lying dead. It seems as if Hauptmann is identifying with Wilhelm and proclaiming his confidence in the younger generation and his trust in the future against all the massive odds of environment and heredity. With an ironic, Wedekind-like shrug of the shoulders, Robert leaves them to it, almost as if he knew that in Hauptmann's next play, *Lonely Lives*, a young couple like Ida and Wilhelm would attempt to make a success of their relationship but that their efforts would end in despair and suicide.

'Lonely Lives'

In his third play, *Lonely Lives* or *Lonely People* (*Einsame Menschen*, 1891), Hauptmann shifts the location to one he knew at first hand. The play takes place in a detached house in Friedrichshagen, on the outskirts of Berlin, the home of a young scientist called Johannes Vockerat and his unassuming wife, Käthe. As the play opens, their first child is being christened to the sound of a harmonium. At once latent tensions surface, for, like most intellectuals of his generation, Johannes does not count himself a Christian and therefore sees his infant son's baptism as a display of religious superstition and a victory for the distaff side of the family and its awesome trinity of church, kitchen and children (*Kirche*, *Küche*, *Kinder*): three words which symbolise the values which the German middle classes were upholding against the onslaughts of scientific progress and liberal thought. The latent tensions in the Vockerat household are exacerbated by the unexpected arrival of an emancipated young woman, Anna Mahr, on the way from her German-speaking home town, Reval (now called Tallinn), in the Russian Baltic province of Estonia, to Zurich, in Switzerland, to continue her studies at the university there, which was one of the first to open its doors to women.

It is soon obvious that Anna has more to offer Johannes than his meek, uneducated wife, who also happens to be recovering from the birth of their child and trying to run the household. A triangular situation seems about to develop along conventional lines, but what is new is that the three persons involved are essentially modern, as are the pressures on them. Anna Mahr was one of the first and most rounded examples in European drama of a new breed of emancipated intellectual woman; of course she owes something to Ibsen's Rebecca West in *Rosmersholm*, a play first performed in Norway and Germany in 1887, but in fact she projects a significantly different type, cosmopolitan, independent, highly motivated and without illusions. She senses the breath of fresh air already blowing in from the twentieth century (as she tells Johannes in Act IV), yet she also realises more clearly than he does that the freedom of thought and action for which they both long is still far off. A homeless outsider herself (her parents were sent to Siberia), she is drawn to the cosy German domesticity of the Vockerats' home, whereas Johannes is drawn to her because he feels stifled by the household's normality and stability, personified in his over-possessive mother and his wife, whose debilitated physical state and intellectual inferiority complex conceal underlying strengths of character which will prove a match even for Anna.

There is no deficiency of love and affection among these people; on the contrary, they do their utmost to understand each other, yet the drama that unfolds reveals with unprecedented clarity a theme which was to become a central one in twentieth-century literature – the basic isolation of all human beings. Their loneliness is accentuated by the efforts they make to overcome it; the occasional, fleeting understandings they reach serve in the long run merely to emphasise their isolation. The most telling example – and a masterpiece of the new psychological realism that Hauptmann was bringing to the stage and which Chekhov admired and was soon to follow up – occurs in Act III as Anna converses with Käthe to fill the time until her train is due to leave:

ANNA. Well, I'm ready. And we still have – how long?

KÄTHE. Three-quarters of an hour at least.

ANNA. Oh, have we? I really have enjoyed staying with you (*taking KÄTHE'S hand*).

KÄTHE. It's gone so quickly.

ANNA. Now I shall go back to Zurich and immerse myself in work. Work, work; that's all I want to do.

KÄTHE. Would you like a sandwich?

ANNA. No, thank you. I couldn't eat anything. (*Pause.*) I'll be glad when all the hellos are over. It's a horrible prospect. All my friends, all asking me...Brrr! (*She shivers as if feeling cold.*) – Will you write to me sometimes?

KÄTHE. If you like, but there's never much to write about here.

ANNA. And will you give me a photograph of yourself?

KÄTHE. Yes, of course (*rummaging through a drawer in the desk*). Here's one; I'm afraid it's rather old.

ANNA (*playfully tapping her on the back of the neck, almost pityingly*). What a thin little neck!

KÄTHE (*turns towards her with a self-deprecating smile*). It hasn't got many brains to support, Anna. Oh, here's a picture (*hands ANNA a photograph*).

ANNA. Oh, that's lovely, it's really lovely. You don't happen to have one of your husband too, do you? I've got so fond of you all.

KÄTHE. I'm not sure that I have.

ANNA. Oh Käthe, do have a look! – Is that one? – That one there?

KÄTHE. Yes, there's one left.

ANNA. Can I have it?

KÄTHE. Yes, Anna, take it.

ANNA (*quickly taking it and putting it in her pocket*). And now you'll all forget all about me. Oh, Käthe! (*She throws her arms round her and bursts into tears.*)

KÄTHE. No, I won't, really, I'll always remember you and...

ANNA. Love me?

KÄTHE. Yes, Anna, of course.

ANNA. Do you really love me?

KÄTHE. What do you mean?

ANNA. Aren't you just a little bit glad I'm going?

KÄTHE. Whatever do you mean?

ANNA (*who has drawn away from KÄTHE again*). It's a good thing I'm going, it really is. Johannes's mother will be glad to see the back of me as well.

KÄTHE. I'm sure that isn't true.

ANNA. No, you'll find I'm right. (*Sitting down at the table.*) Oh, what's the point? (*Forgetting herself, she takes out the photograph and gazes at it intently.*) He has such deep lines round his mouth.

37

KÄTHE. Who has?

ANNA. Hannes. Such sad lines. That comes from being alone.
People who are alone have so much to put up with from
other people – How did you come to know each other?

KÄTHE. Oh, it was...

ANNA. Was he still a student?

KÄTHE. Yes, he was.

ANNA. And you were very young, and you just said yes?

KÄTHE (*blushing with embarrassment*). Not exactly...

ANNA (*emotionally*). Oh, Käthe, Käthe. (*She puts the photo
away again and rises.*) Isn't it time yet?

KÄTHE. No, there's still plenty of time.

ANNA. Plenty? Oh, God, is there still plenty of time? (*She
sits down at the piano.*) You don't play, do you? (*KÄTHE
shakes her head.*) And you don't sing either? (*KÄTHE shakes
her head again.*) And yet Hannes is so fond of music, isn't
he? – I used to play, and I used to sing too. But it's a long
time ago. (*Getting up abruptly.*) Still, never mind.

Anna does not catch her train. She lingers, allowing herself to
be persuaded by Johannes to stay on in Berlin. But it is already
autumn, and time is running out. Although he is unable to face
the prospect of being separated from the only person he thinks
can understand him and truly value his scientific research,
Johannes complies with his parents' insistence that she should
leave. In doing so, he places duty to his wife and family above
his much-vaunted duty to himself, but the outcome is not the
happy end with which most Victorian playwrights would have
rewarded him. Tense, highly strung, self-indulgent even,
Johannes is finally drawn to the nearby lake, in which he
presumably drowns himself as the play comes to a disturbing
and inconclusive end to the sound of frantic cries and the
confused movements of people searching in the dark by the light
of lanterns. Käthe is left all alone to face up to the responsibilities

of bringing up their child by herself; ironically, her reluctance to shoulder any responsibility and her readiness to defer to his better judgement had been a source of irritation and misunderstanding right from the start of the play and had been a major underlying reason for his alienation from her. The ending, with its anticipation of the one-parent family, sheds ironic light on the themes of self-fulfilment and female emancipation represented by Anna Mahr.

Johannes quotes Anna to Käthe in Act II: 'Anna's absolutely right. None of you can see any further than the kitchen and the nursery. There's nothing beyond, as far as German women are concerned.' Käthe is quick to reply, 'But somebody has to do the cooking and look after the children. It's all very well for her to talk like that. I'd rather sit and read books too....' The issue is one that has been endlessly debated during the last hundred years, but when these exchanges between a modern young husband and his wife were first heard by audiences in Berlin early in 1891, their topicality was startling. However, *Lonely Lives* is not just a play of ideas; it is a subtle, sensitively crafted exploration of complex relationships developing between three characters conceived in the round. They make use of ideas current at the time in order to express their needs and longings and because such views seemed to promise satisfactory answers to some of the personal, moral and social dilemmas facing thinking people like themselves. Johannes sees in Anna Mahr a release from the restrictions and routine of late-nineteenth-century middle-class life, while in her eyes he represents the comfortable stability of an ordered existence. Both are probably mistaken, as Käthe instinctively knows; but she, too, is powerless to avert the outcome. The play is clearly of its time, and is all too easy to underrate for that reason. But loneliness and non-communication, its central themes, are still very much part of our social and psychological climate, which suggests that the play is still highly relevant. There can be no doubt that, in giving it the title it bears, Hauptmann foreshadowed many of the major writers of the twentieth century.

'The Weavers'

Gerhart Hauptmann's most famous play soon established itself as the classic dramatic portrayal of the working class. Kaiser Wilhelm II disapproved of it; Lenin gave instructions for its clandestine publication and circulation in Russia in a translation by his own sister and edited by himself. It has remained the outstanding example of its genre ever since, and its influence may be traced in many documentaries of our own day and in contemporary dramatisations of social unrest, uprising and organised repression.

With *The Weavers* (*Die Weber*, 1893) Hauptmann took the decisive step of presenting on stage without comment something which leading contemporaries, foremost among them Zola, had been bringing to the attention of the public in the form of meticulously researched realistic novels. The result created a new concept of drama. As Brecht later observed, Naturalist drama such as this evolved out of the novels of Zola and Dostoyevsky and was itself the starting-point for epic drama as he conceived it. In order to make the new type of subject matter associated with such novels suitable for the stage, Hauptmann developed a discursive dramatic form similar to theirs. This dramatic form has become so much part of our theatrical experience that it is hard to appreciate the immense aesthetic revolution which *The Weavers* represented when, after difficulties with the censors, it was premièred in Berlin in a closed performance given by the Freie Bühne on 26 February 1893. After numerous further police bans and legal proceedings (some of which went on until 1901), the first public performance of the play finally took place on 25 September 1894 in the Deutsches Theater, Berlin, which had just been taken over by Otto Brahm. By this time a French translation by Jean Thorel entitled *Les Tisserands* had been mounted at the Théâtre Libre, André Antoine's pioneering stage-company in Paris, in the presence of Zola himself.

In Germany, meanwhile, expectations had been roused by the play's first published edition, available in both the original dialect version entitled *De Waber*, and in a more easily readable version closer to standard German by Hauptmann himself. Supporters and critics of the play formed two steadily growing and vociferous opposing groups, while the printed texts made it clear that the author was intent on dragging the theatre into a new age. The meticulous instructions he provides for the settings of each of the five acts indicate plainly that these are no longer stage-sets in the traditional sense: they are locations designed to create total authenticity and bring home the inescapable influence of environment on human attitudes and behaviour. This, one of the central tenets of the Naturalist movement, is something which we now tend to take for granted, with the result that what Hauptmann regarded as an essential aspect of his drama often tends to be played down in modern productions in favour of a more stylised, 'timeless' approach or of a didactic, distanced Brechtian presentation.

What Hauptmann seems to have had in mind from the start was in fact a sort of period piece, a reconstruction or re-creation of what life was really like in Silesia fifty years earlier when a weavers' uprising had actually taken place; in 1891 he made two fact-finding visits to the region in order to get the feel of the place and interview eyewitnesses of the events he was dramatising. The first public production, in 1894, went beyond his intentions, however. While admiring the 'artistic objectivity' of the play above all, the producer, his friend Otto Brahm, laid particular emphasis on the weavers' plight by playing down both their shortcomings and the manufacturers' redeeming features.

As a result, the audience was roused to near-hysteria at the sight of such blatant economic exploitation of downtrodden, vulnerable victims. Contemporary reviewers also commented on the way in which *The Weavers* broke down the conventional barrier between actors and audience. A new concept of drama had indeed emerged. Meanwhile the play's political repercussions added a further topical dimension. It was given ninety-three performances during its first season, but the Kaiser was deeply offended and gave up his box at the theatre. This brought notoriety, increased box-office takings, and pointed unmistakably to the topical relevance of the historical events on which Hauptmann had based his proletarian tragedy without a hero.

The Weavers is based on events which took place in a number of small textile-manufacturing towns in Silesia in the 1840s, when foreign competition, largely from Lancashire, led to a fall in demand and prices, and brought the local cottage industry to crisis point because its handlooms were unable to compete with the new machinery abroad. The action of the play is thus contemporaneous with the working-class deprivations and industrial conflicts depicted by Mrs Gaskell in her pioneering Manchester novels, *Mary Barton* and *North and South*. During the intervening fifty years European novelists had been developing ways of describing the basic tensions in industrialised society as change becomes inevitable. But no playwright had managed to devise an equally effective scenic presentation, capable of bringing out the complexity of the underlying trends and issues and showing not just individuals but whole communities in conflict: a type of play in which the protagonist (if there is one) is a whole class of people, not just one individual, and the villain (if villain there be) is the influence of market forces and social attitudes. The notion of social drama was in the air at the time; Hauptmann now rose to the challenge by taking it a decisive step beyond the concept forcefully exemplified by Ibsen in plays such as *An Enemy of the People* (first performed in Oslo in 1883). He realised that the result would offend the Establishment by reviving uncomfortable memories, and that his dramatisation of incidents fifty years ago, if dramatically successful, would come to influence people's mental picture of the industrial age. This is exactly what happened: the images he created – the boy collapsing with hunger at the feet of his employer, the family unable to eat even dog-meat because it is too rich for them, the crowd timidly gaping at the manufacturer's luxurious furnishings after they have broken into his house – images and incidents such as these have worked their way into the general consciousness and can be seen reflected and repeated in countless treatments of similar situations on stage, and of course in films and television.

The lead given by *The Weavers* demonstrates the degree to which Hauptmann's creative imagination and stagecraft had outstripped those of his contemporaries. Its impact outside Germany may clearly be seen when it is compared with *Strife*, the best-known play by John Galsworthy (1867–1933). Galsworthy always denied he had any first-hand knowledge of Hauptmann's play (though the fine English version of it by Mary Morison had been published in London by Heinemann in 1899), but *Strife*, first produced at the Duke of York's Theatre, London, on 1 March 1909, contains many similarities to *The Weavers*. Both plays chart the parabola of an industrial dispute, and in both of them the setting of the first act – a room in the employer–manufacturer's house – is contrasted in Act II with a graphic picture of the living conditions endured by his working-class employees. In *The Weavers* this room is narrow and low, with rotting floorboards and soot-blackened rafters; two frail girls with thin, bare shoulders sit working their looms while their mother, prematurely bent and aged and with a face as emaciated as a skeleton's sits at a spinning-wheel, as does her son, a half-wit with stunted body and gangling limbs. In *Strife* the room is clean and tidy, whitewashed but much stained with smoke; a thin, dark-haired woman with patient eyes sits in an old armchair by a meagre little fire; other women are there too, one of them small, pale, pinched-up, the other old and ashen-white, while young Madge Thomas listens to their talk. In both plays the talk at this point is mainly about food or, rather, the lack of it, and undertones of anxiety are unmistakable.

Where the two plays differ is equally telling. *Strife*, a play in three acts, works towards a resolution: the workers at the Trenartha Tin Plate Works decide to fight on, and their resolve is met almost half-way by their employers' decision to concede most of their demands. Mutual respect emerges at the end from a painful situation which need never have arisen in the first place. Hauptmann's play follows a similar course of events, but draws less comforting conclusions. The dispute between the weavers and their employers escalates, their half-baked political aspirations are stoked by trouble-makers, and open violence ensues. They break into their paymaster's house and, in response, the forces of law and order are called out to deal with them; firearms are used in a street battle, and the strikers' jubilant shouts of victory coincide jarringly with the death of an old weaver, Hilse, struck by a stray bullet. Is this a comment on the events, and thus an authorial intrusion out of keeping with the Naturalist objectivity of the play? If so, what are its implications? The ending of *The Weavers* has provoked much discussion, but in strictly dramatic terms its significance is bold and clear: compared to the ending of *Strife*, with its blend of stage effectiveness and pretentiously ironic curtain line, Hauptmann's ending conveys the arbitrariness of life as well as its continuity. This is entirely in keeping with the Naturalist doctrine that a play can never be more than a 'slice of life', and that effective *dénouements* to contrived plots are the enemy of true drama.

The impact of *The Weavers* on twentieth-century drama has been far-reaching, and its influence on cinema and television probably even greater. The degree to which Hauptmann's masterpiece in the Naturalist manner anticipated later developments in technique and stylistic approach may be seen if the original text of the play, complete with all its circumstantially detailed stage-directions, is compared with the film version of it which was made over thirty years later, in 1927. This is widely regarded as one of the finest achievements of the silent cinema (the director was F. Zelnik), yet it seems antiquated alongside Hauptmann's blueprint for the treatment of this type of subject matter, not least because it lacks the vital aural dimension which was so important to him. Equally interesting is the part which Hauptmann's dramatic depiction of a social situation at crisis point was later to have in the emergence of socialist realism in the Soviet Union and elsewhere. Lenin had been quick to realise that *The Weavers* was accessible to the broad mass of people and that it was a work of art to which workers could easily and naturally relate; his personal interest in the first Russian translation and its circulation helped the play to become a classic of committed working-class art and ensured a respected place for Hauptmann in the new post-Revolutionary literary canon, as well as the protection of the Red Army when Silesia was taken in 1945.

The Silesian plays

The original and more authentic version of *The Weavers* was called *De Waber*, and was written in the German dialect of the part of Silesia where the events of the drama actually took place and which Hauptmann knew at first hand. His home territory was to provide the setting for many of his most convincing plays in the realistic manner. In Germany two of these, *Drayman*

Henschel (*Fuhrmann Henschel*, 1898) and *Rose Bernd* (1903), are regarded as masterpieces of modern drama. Obstinately they have remained plays limited to home consumption.

Shortly after *The Weavers*, Hauptmann wrote another play with a Silesian setting. This was *Hannele's Assumption* (*Hanneles Himmelfahrt*), one of his most controversial stageworks. First performed in Berlin on 14 September 1893, Hauptmann's 'dream play' had within a year been translated into English by the drama critic William Archer and performed in French at the Théâtre Libre. It opens in a poorhouse in some small mountain town on a bitter December night. The inmates quarrel, gamble and joke with one another; suddenly they are interrupted by the arrival of the village schoolmaster carrying a fourteen-year-old girl who has been rescued from suicide by drowning. The play revolves round this girl, Hannele, a pathetic case of child abuse. But audiences were in for a surprise. Instead of highlighting her case in order to demonstrate the negative effects of heredity and environment and call society to show concern or blame it for letting such things happen, Hauptmann set out to explore deeper levels and reveal less easily tangible dimensions. In her delirium Hannele imagines she can see and hear her stepfather bullying her; the hallucination evaporates as a nurse returns to soothe her to sleep; then *'a dim light fills the desolate room, and on the edge of the bed, bending forward and supporting herself on her thin, bare arms, sits a pale, ghostly woman'*. From this point on, the play oscillates increasingly between the down-to-earth 'real' world represented by the poorhouse, in which one of society's child victims is ill and dying, and the imagined world in which she thinks she is and which is more real to her, a world which is of course really just a projection of her delirium. In that world, snatches of Sunday-school hymn and nursery fairy-tale merge with memories of her dead mother and with the traumas of the sufferings she has since endured, and create a vision of

Gerhart Hauptmann

Heaven as seen by a deprived girl in the late nineteenth century.

Hannele's heaven is cloyingly sentimental at times, hopelessly muddled, its sincerely naïve Christianity contaminated by kitsch and inspired by her adolescent crush on the village schoolmaster, who has at least attempted to be kind to her. Her deprived and insecure home background and her debilitated physical condition are of course both responsible for her visions: the play remains true to its author's Naturalist beliefs. But theatrically it bursts the barriers of realism. Not only does it proclaim the equal validity and importance of what is going on in Hannele's mind; it also finds ways of rendering her delirious mental pictures visible. Since what she sees is itself confused and distorted, the play, which had begun in an uncompromisingly realistic manner, soon enters the as yet undiscovered country of Expressionism and indeed Surrealism.

Hauptmann was convinced that Freud (1856–1939) owed more than a little to this dramatic venture into the subconscious, and Strindberg (1849–1912), who was in Berlin at the time of the play's first performances, was to take up the idea and bring it to further fruition in his *A Dream Play* of 1902, which deliberately sets out to imitate the disconnected logic of dreams as Hauptmann's *Hannele* had done. When Basil Dean's production of *Hannele* was given at the Liverpool Playhouse in 1912–13, Gertrude Lawrence and Noël Coward both appeared in it as angels in the beatific vision that accompanies Hannele's death, or, rather, her liberation from the squalor and misery of the nineteenth-century world in which she eked out her brief, insignificant life. The stage-directions that follow this climax are particularly interesting from the technical point of view and vividly convey the novelty of Hauptmann's stagecraft:

While the angels are singing the stage becomes darker. Out of the darkness their singing can be heard growing fainter and fainter, further and further away. It gradually becomes

*light again: before us is the room in the poorhouse, where
everything is exactly as it was before* HANNELE's *first
hallucination.* HANNELE *is seen again lying in bed, poor sick
child.* DR WACHLER *is bending over her with his stethoscope;
the nurse, holding a lamp for him, watches him anxiously.
The sound of the singing now dies away completely.*

DR WACHLER (*straightening up*). You are right.

SISTER MARTHA (*questioningly*). Dead?

DR WACHLER (*nods sadly*). Dead.

Hannele occupies an important position in German theatrical
history. Hauptmann's first play, *Before Sunrise*, had
disconcerted German audiences with its new realism and forced
producers and actors to abandon histrionics and adopt true-to-
life speech, gestures, costumes and settings. Now, less than four
years later, *Hannele* invited 'Naturalist' actors and producers
to go beyond social verisimilitude and psychological realism
and enter a new world of stylised movement and magical
incantation in which down-to-earth dialect is gently drowned
by the lilting rhythms and fanciful imagery of verse. This was
a pointer to future developments. It indicated that, for all his
uncompromising social realism, Hauptmann also possessed a
strong impulse to explore the fantasy world of dream and make-
believe. Henceforth a large proportion of what he wrote was
to be in this domain, though he always retained his sure grasp
of the realist mode and kept both feet on the ground, theatrically
speaking. *Hannele*, however, pointed the way towards the play
which turned out to be far and away his most popular work in
German-speaking countries before 1914: *The Sunken Bell* (*Die
versunkene Glocke*), first performed in Berlin in 1896.

It is significant that this foray into fairy-tale, which appealed
so inordinately to German middle-class audiences, flopped when
it was staged in Paris: clearly this type of Teutonic escapism
was not to the French taste. It did not catch on in Britain either,

though its 1899 English translation by Charles Henry Meltzer (who also translated *Hannele*) was frequently staged and reprinted in the United States. In Germany the play's reception was rapturous. People avidly read and discussed the text – comparisons with Goethe's *Faust* were ventured! – and the first edition ran to twenty-one impressions in the first six months, with a thousand copies in each. The success of the first Berlin production was enhanced by the fact that two of Germany's greatest actors, Josef Kainz and Agnes Sorma, created the leading roles. Today it may seem an inferior play, and no doubt most of the innumerable productions of it mounted in Germany before 1914 bordered on the fey; yet the distinguished drama critic Julius Bab (1880–1955) recalled that there was not a hint of kitsch when Agnes Sorma perched on the edge of her woodland well, combing her auburn hair and warding off an inquisitive bee: 'her eyes glistened like blades of grass in the sunlight and darted dangerous glances like those of a spitting cat'. When American audiences saw Miss Sorma in the part of the elfin Rautendelein, they agreed. Who would have thought that the elusive blue flower of German Romanticism would spring up so soon on the dung-heap of Naturalism?

Meanwhile Hauptmann continued to write plays in the realistic vein with which he was so closely associated, exploring the characters and changing relationships of uniquely ordinary people living out their humdrum lives in the particular circumstances of a specific time and place. One of the finest of these later social dramas is *Drayman Henschel*, which opened on 5 November 1898 at the Deutsches Theater, Berlin, with Rudolf Rittner in the title part and Else Lehmann, Germany's greatest exponent of Naturalist acting and the creator of Helene Krause, in the part of Hanne Schäl, the strapping young woman who becomes the drayman's second wife with the most disastrous results. Their incompatible relationship unfolds below stairs in a hotel at a Silesian spa during the 1860s: in other words the play re-creates the environment in which the author grew up. Seen in retrospect, it was a period of change, and Henschel becomes its victim because the horse-drawn vehicles on which he depends for his living become obsolete with the arrival of the railway. The play is rooted in the precisely recalled reality of time and place, while at its centre the once-commanding personality of Henschel the drayman disintegrates before our eyes as he turns into an elderly and disorientated man made redundant by progress and deceived by his young wife. It is a tragic drama of almost ancient-Greek intensity, powerful and brooding, and – as Thomas Mann observed – as timeless in its way as the Oresteian myths, to which Hauptmann, as an old man harrowed by the horrors of the Second World War, turned in his last plays. The example of the drayman, hounded to suicide in a setting of claustrophobic, suffocating domesticity, was not lost on Hauptmann's most enthusiastic American admirer, Eugene O'Neill (1888–1953), whose brooding, passionate drama *Desire under the Elms* (1924) has a great deal in common with it.

1903 saw the first performance in Berlin of Hauptmann's other great Silesian social drama, *Rose Bernd*, with Else Lehmann in the title role (taken later by Ethel Barrymore in a notable production at the Longacre Theater on Broadway in 1922, where it ran for ten weeks). The play is in a sense complementary to *Drayman Henschel*, but the tragic victim is now the strapping girl herself. Good-natured and uncomplicated, Rose is the girlfriend of Christoph Flamm, a local landowner and magistrate, an outgoing man almost twice her age who happens to be married to an invalid. They like each other; nature has its way and takes its course. But these human beings are unable to accept the life-force in them openly and frankly: convention, respectability and, worse, embarrassment and crippling shame make Rose's father insist she wed a pious young man who is in no way suited to being her sexual partner, and make Rose herself the easy victim of an arrogant mechanic who blackmails her, and whose job servicing the new-fangled farming machines gives him notoriety and sexual appeal among the country folk. Caught between the men surrounding her, rather like Tess of the d'Urbervilles in Hardy's novel of 1891, Rose Bernd lacks the instinct for self-preservation. Unable to extricate herself from her situation, she becomes the victim of circumstances. Her arrest at the end, after she has killed her baby, is open-ended – a clear rejection of a theatrically effective *dénouement* for its own sake, and at the same time an implicit plea for understanding and compassion: Hauptmann had recently swayed a jury to acquit a girl caught in similar circumstances, and was eager to share the insights he had gained from this encounter with a real-life human tragedy which had appalled him.

Rose Bernd is more of a *pièce à thèse* than Hauptmann's plays usually are, but it puts its plea for compassion forward tactfully and indirectly. Dramatically it is a *tour de force*. It opens memorably (Hauptmann was by now a master of exposition) with Rose and her lover, Flamm, emerging bashfully from the bushes, then bursting into happy laughter together. The action generated by what has just taken place follows the steady course of the seasons from that first clear, sunny May morning through the scorching harvest days of high summer to an autumnal evening in September, the mood of each act being sensitively conditioned by the time of year. The play reaches its greatest intensity with the fight that breaks out between August Keil, Rose's weedy fiancé, and Streckmann, the bullying mechanic, out in the fields at harvest time one sultry August afternoon.

Another telling aspect of *Rose Bernd* is the use within a strictly Naturalist context of techniques associated with the new French drama of the unspoken, whose leading exponent, Maurice Maeterlinck (1862–1949), had been becoming increasingly popular during the late 1890s. In line with these new developments, decisive events to which the action would normally be expected to build up are relegated to the intervals of time which elapse between one act and the next, while the 'action' presented on stage becomes an exploration of the multiple, conflicting responses of the characters to what has happened or may happen, a technical development in line with Hauptmann's dictum, 'What you add to your plot, you subtract from your characters.' What was unusual and in its way revolutionary was the application of this approach not to the articulate, sophisticated sort of people favoured by other dramatists, but to German country folk, people generally considered to be lacking in psychological complexity. By the end of the play, words themselves completely fail Hauptmann's finest Naturalist heroine: her tragic experience takes place on a level beyond the reach of words, and words, however sincere and urgent, are quite unable to express it. Instead, the inevitable logic of the dramatic build-up and the audience's absorption in it make Rose's tragedy almost palpable; our emotions respond, and our minds may become more sympathetic to similar tragedies in real life. *Rose Bernd* was the confirmation of its author's belief that all men and women are psychologically complex and have tragic potential, regardless of their social status and the language they speak.

The Berlin plays

Though he was deeply attached to the rural world of Silesia, Hauptmann knew that Berlin was where the challenge lay. With his early plays he had gone a long way towards conquering its more thoughtful and discriminating public, and his excursion into the neo-Romantic world of fairy-tale had proved a box-office success. With *The Weavers* finished and let loose on the world, he decided to make the capital city of the new united Germany into the setting for plays presenting some of its most pressing social and human problems. Berlin was growing at an unprecedented rate, comparable only to the cities of the United States: in 1800 it had had a population of 170,000, but by 1890 it had 1,580,000 inhabitants. It had doubled in size between 1875 and 1910, and when Hauptmann came to write his Berlin plays it ranked third in size among the major cities of Europe.

After a projected Berlin novel which came to nothing, he set about exploring the dramatic potential of Germany's 'big city'. The Berlin plays which resulted have never been surpassed, as is shown by their continuing popularity among German audiences even after the Second World War, which witnessed the partition of Berlin and its loss of the metropolitan status it had enjoyed during the period when he was writing. Nostalgia may well have replaced the indignation and shock which the Berlin plays aroused when they were first performed, but it remains true to say that in the German-speaking world today Hauptmann's reputation as a major playwright rests largely on *The Beaver Coat* (*Der Biberpelz*, 1893) and *Rats* (*Die Ratten*, 1911). These two plays were performed 3995 and 2331 times respectively between 1947 and 1975 in the Federal Republic of Germany.

The Beaver Coat is one of the relatively few successful comedies to have been written for the German stage, and the performance figures speak for its popularity. Like Hauptmann's serious plays, it has not travelled well. Sporadic attempts have been made to stage it in Britain, for instance at the Court Theatre, London, in 1905, when it ran for nine performances; at the Gaiety Theatre, Manchester, where it was put on by the enterprising Horniman Company in 1912; and at the People's Theatre, Newcastle-upon-Tyne, in 1942. Its failure to catch on outside Germany is probably due to the tendency of non-Germans to see it either as a portrayal of typically German attitudes or as a satire on them, rather than as the masterly and exceedingly comic account it actually is of human nature in action in what happens to be a Berlin setting. Hauptmann subtitled *The Beaver Coat* a 'thieves' comedy', and caused further consternation at the first performance (at the Deutsches Theater, Berlin, on 21 September 1893) by deliberately bringing the curtain down on Act IV, thus depriving the audience of the reassuringly conventional and morally satisfying *dénouement* they had been expecting, in which everything should of course be set right and the guilty receive due punishment. Alas, in *The Beaver Coat* this is not the case. Hauptmann's central character, the ebullient and indomitable Frau Wolff, a washerwoman by trade, manages to navigate every comic hurdle and survives every farcical setback – indeed, survival is the dominant theme in Hauptmann's Berlin plays and reflects his admiration for the instinctive ability of so many ordinary Berliners to cope with the pressures and problems of modern urban life, from unemployment and social deprivation to the uncaring ineptitude and stuffy red tape of officialdom and the Establishment.

Frau Wolff embodies this spirit of survival: indeed, she may even be said to embody the spirit of Berlin. Of course, she is sadly lacking in moral scruples, but she is nothing if not human, all too human. She is a full-blooded character after Dickens' own heart, which may paradoxically be another reason why she has never managed to endear herself to English-speaking audiences; for, naturally enough, her personality emerges through her behaviour and above all her way of speaking, and this in turn is rooted in her background and environment. To German ears this is immediately audible; Frau Wolff's repartee is an inimitable expression of herself – an astute though uneducated woman of Silesian origin long resident in one of the outer suburbs of Berlin. She was in fact drawn very much from life. Herr von Wehrhahn, the Kaiser-worshipping local magistrate, is no match for such a woman. Incompetent and arrogant, he is only concerned with apprehending left-wing agitators in the person of young Dr Fleischer, a lukewarm liberal. Crime detection is not Herr von Wehrhahn's strongest point, and he ludicrously fails to realise that his trusty washerwoman and the purloiner of the beaver coat are of course one and the same person, or indeed that the stolen coat is in fact the very one that its honest-looking rogue of a recipient has openly been wearing. So many people of all classes seem to possess fur coats nowadays!

The Beaver Coat is a celebration of the individual and a light-hearted send-up of the restrictions and regulations people have to put up with, which are at one and the same time social necessities and symbolic of the impersonal system against which the individual has to pit his wits. As Herr von Wehrhahn patronisingly observes in Frau Wolff's presence at the end of the comedy,

> This lady here is our hard-working washerwoman. She thinks that all people are like her. But unfortunately, Frau Wolff, that isn't how things are in this world. You look at people from the outside: people like myself look a bit deeper. And when I tell you that Frau Wolff is an honest soul, that's as true as when I say that Dr Fleischer is an extremely dangerous fellow.

Frau Wolff has the last word, of course. With a resigned shake of her head she comments, 'Well, I don't know....'

In 1950-1 Brecht and his ensemble produced an adaptation of *The Beaver Coat* and its sequel, *The Conflagration* (*Der rote Hahn*, 1901), a less light-hearted comedy in which Frau Wolff, now called Frau Fielitz, sets fire to her husband's shoe-shop in order to claim the insurance money and climb still further up in the world. Brecht's conflation of Hauptmann's two Berlin comedies spells out the social and political issues involved, but this proves counter-productive because, once Frau Wolff is presented as the product of a defective social system rather than as a fully developed character in her own right, our sympathy for her tends to diminish, and this in turn blunts the satirical bite of the unholy war she wages against our far-from-perfect world. By 1893 Hauptmann was well enough versed in the tenets and techniques of Naturalism to know that we are all of us determined by environment, heredity and the pressures of the moment, and to know how these factors can be subtly built into the dialogue and stage-sets of a play. He also knew how to use them to comic and even farcical effect. In this he was expertly backed up by the actress who created the role of Frau Wolff and made it very much her own – Else Lehmann. It was up to producers and actors to take his hints, and to his readers and spectators to draw their own conclusions. The didactic strain so evident in Brecht was totally absent from his make-up.

Rats is the finest play ever to have been written about Berlin; some call it Hauptmann's masterpiece. First performed on 13 January 1911 at the Lessing-Theater, Berlin, it brings together a rich multiplicity of autobiographical and topical themes to capture the essence of Berlin and the feel of what life in the city was like for ordinary people back in the early years of the century. The play's underlying idea, Hauptmann said, is the contrast between two worlds; these two worlds are the ones of the play's two main characters: Frau Henriette John, a mason's wife and a woman of the people, and Harro Hassenreuter, a retired theatrical director, whose ambience is the glamorous yet rather shabby amalgam of culture, good living, and getting-by which characterises most people's view of life in a capital city. The worlds of these two characters coincide, however, because they both inhabit the same converted barracks in Berlin's east end; there Frau John lives out her humdrum life in her tidy little flat, while Herr Hassenreuter rents a dusty old attic above, in which he stores his theatrical properties and costumes and gives private coaching to would-be actors. Around these two

characters and their settting, a complex, many-stranded tragi-
comedy develops which is simultaneously concerned with the
fate of a Polish immigrant worker's illegitimate baby and the
destiny of the German Empire. And throughout the play rats
are gnawing away behind the skirting-boards and underneath
the floor of the teeming tenement house, which gradually
becomes a symbol of a whole nation and its capital city.

Frau John (pronounced to rhyme with 'own') would
desperately like to have a baby, and buys the Polish girl's
unwanted one. Of course, she would give it a better start in
life and probably love it more, but her pathetic attempt to achieve
motherhood falls foul of the social services, which in Bismarck's
Germany had begun to foreshadow the welfare state of the later
twentieth century. The whole illicit business comes to light
because, ironically, the Polish girl, though almost illiterate in
German, is dutiful and guileless enough to register the baby's
birth in her own name. In her distress, Frau John seeks the help
of her delinquent and backward brother, Bruno; he does what
he can and bumps the girl off behind some lilac bushes. That
is one strand of the drama, and its ending is a tragic one. Fearing
that she will be found out, punished, and deprived of the child,
Frau John panics and rushes out to kill herself by hurling herself
down into the busy street below.

While Frau John is experiencing her short-lived happiness
and descent into tragic despair, Herr Hassenreuter endeavours
to instil the rudiments of classical drama into his small group
of pupils, one of whom, Spitta, till recently a theology student,
is an ardent adherent of modern Naturalism and social
verisimilitude. In Act III, as Frau John comes to clean the
premises with mop and bucket, Hassenreuter points at her with
histrionic gesture and tells him, 'Here comes your tragic muse!'
The others burst out laughing, and the poor embarrassed woman
asks, 'What's so funny about me?' The irony is that, like young
Spitta, the well-meaning intellectual, she is quite unaware of

her tragic potential, whereas Herr Hassenreuter, in spite of all his posturing and bluster, has just enough human sympathy and genuine culture to perceive it, though only when it is already too late.

What makes *Rats* particularly interesting as a contribution to early-twentieth-century theatre is that it is at one and the same time a play about people, a social study, and a probing inquiry into the nature of modern drama. Indeed, it is Hauptmann's central statement on the subject, deliberately presented in dramatic form rather than as a theoretical exposé or a polemical preface in the manner of Shaw. In a hilarious scene in Act III (i.e. right at the centre of this five-act play), Hassenreuter rehearses his hopeful pupils Kegel, Käferstein and Spitta in a chorus from Schiller's most stylised verse tragedy *The Bride of Messina* (*Die Braut von Messina*, 1803). Its sonorous words and high-flown diction are totally and preposterously out of place in his dusty attic, yet curiously relevant to such dark and dismal surroundings: the discrepancy is irresistibly funny, but also prompts the question which T. S. Eliot was later to consider – are verse and poetic diction still feasible as a medium for drama when the playwright, even the serious one, is concerned with modern problems and his play is set in the recognisable world of today? Human problems are of course eternal – Frau John's goes back to the days of Solomon – but modern realism has steadily and inevitably reduced the upper range of language, which used to be considered essential to tragic drama, and in its place has opened up that whole vast, uncharted area where articulate speech gives way to aposiopesis and anacoluthon or is replaced by grunts, sighs, expletives and other paralinguistic signals – an expressive area memorably represented in *Rats* by Frau John's cat-like delinquent brother, whose crude Berlin underworld slang is about as far removed from Schiller's verse as it is possible to be. Linguistically the range of the play is indeed enormous; it covers the whole of spoken drama from high tragedy to kitchen sink. Sociologically it spans an equally wide spectrum, from the criminal underworld of big-city crime and drug abuse to Herr Hassenreuter's much-vaunted aristocratic connections, appropriately invisible off stage. It is graphically realistic down to the last detail. Yet so permeated with irony is this great work of Hauptmann's maturity that in subtle, sensitive performance its superficial realism is forever disintegrating, like the society it depicts, and we find ourselves wondering whether what we are witnessing is a hidden allegory or a grim, sardonic farce.

The artist in the theatre

The private problems of the creative artist and his public role are a constant theme of modern German literature, and it is not surprising that they surface in the works of Hauptmann and his contemporaries. The figure of the painter Schwarz in *Earth Spirit*, the first of Wedekind's two Lulu plays, reveals the risks run by the artist as he treads the tightrope between the insatiable demands of modern materialist society and his own inner creative vision, while that of the writer Alwa Schön in the Lulu plays reveals the weakness as well as the strength which arises from the artist's ability to observe life from the outside, often at the price of losing it in the very act of capturing it. In Schnitzler's case, it could be said that Anatol lives life like an artist, improvising as he goes along; elsewhere, in one-acters such as *Literature*, writers actually figure as central characters in plays whose actions turn on the susceptibilities and vagaries of the artistic personality.

But it was Hauptmann who achieved the greatest distinction in his dramatic presentation of the theme of the artist. At various points in his career he wrote plays which focus on it. His early comedy *Colleague Crampton* (*Kollege Crampton*, 1892), based on his own experience as an art student, is an amusing but at the same time touching, even disturbing portrayal of a provincial art-school lecturer who once had artistic potential and now drowns his incompetence in drink, but who actually possesses greater artistic insight than most of his shallow students and colleagues. The later play *Peter Brauer* (not published until 1921) is a tragi-comedy at the expense of the artist, or, rather, the Germanic tendency to take artists almost too seriously: commissioned by a wealthy Silesian aristocrat to paint frescoes in the family chapel, Brauer only manages to produce garden gnomes. Not surprisingly, the play has never gone down well in Germany!

In between these two relatively light-hearted treatments of the theme, Hauptmann created two profoundly serious, indeed tragic studies of the agony that results from the gaping discrepancy between the artist's vision and the stifling claims and petty distractions of the everyday world which no artist can ever escape, because life provides the emotional content of art as well as its subject-matter.

Gabriel Schilling's Flight (*Gabriel Schillings Flucht*), first produced before a select audience in a small spa town near Weimar in 1912, subtly interfuses a crisis in an artist's creativity with his gradual disintegration as his diabetes reaches crisis point (this, of course, was before the discovery of insulin). In a desperate attempt to escape the confines of unhealthy, built-up Berlin and the strains of a disastrous marriage and an equally destructive affair with another woman, Schilling goes to earth on an island in the Baltic. But when he is tracked down by his worn-out harridan of a wife and by Hanna Elias, his highly strung, harpy-like mistress, the island becomes a place of death for him, even though for others, such as the young violinist Lucie Heil and her extrovert boyfriend, the sculptor Mäurer, it is a sun-drenched, ozone-filled earthly paradise. The atmospheric qualities of the play are extraordinary – not as wistful as J. M. Barrie's mysterious island drama *Mary Rose* (1920), it captures the radiance, the bracing climate and the *joie de vivre* of its Baltic setting, but also that underlying menace and melancholy more readily associated with the portraits and seascapes of Scandinavian painters of the period. The cinema rather than the stage would be the medium to do it justice.

The themes of flight and pursuit, of possessiveness, self-preservation and emotional blackmail predominate over the existential crisis of an artist in Hauptmann's fascinating experiment in reconciling the tormented psychological domain of Strindberg with the delicacy of Chekhov – an influence acknowledged in many a touch, from symbolical seagulls to the amusing take-off of a young Russian woman in Fräulein Majakin, inspired, like much of the play, by Hauptmann's friends and his own affair with Ida Orloff, which had come to an end in 1906 on a Baltic island. But the artistic predicament is central to *Michael Kramer*, his masterpiece in the 'artist-drama' genre. First produced on 21 December 1900 at the Deutsches Theater, Berlin, with Max Reinhardt in the title role, and still successfully revived from time to time in German-speaking countries, *Michael Kramer* draws its dramatic tension from the love–hate relationship between a father and a son unable to bridge the generation gap, yet both committed to the single-minded pursuit of an artistic ideal. Kramer, an artist of the old school, earns just enough in a provincial academy to spend all his spare time in solitary vigil in his studio, working on his painting of the suffering Christ, a canvas all the more effective as a stage prop because it is never actually seen. Meanwhile, in the modern city outside, his talented son, Arnold, a prototype of the mid-century outsider, sketches obnoxious, vulgar, self-made middle-class men, who take revenge by ridiculing the young satirist and goading him to suicide.

Alone with the body of his son, Kramer expresses his grief and insight into the meaning of suffering and death and their relation to beauty and love in a sequence of groping, hesitant monologues which build up into a glowing personal expression of faith which won the admiration of both the poet Rilke and the young novelist James Joyce, who translated the play into English within a year of its publication and built allusions to it into *Dubliners* (1914) and *A Portrait of the Artist as a Young Man* (1914). The admiration of such major fellow writers is not surprising. The play's persuasive suggestion that genius is akin to failure and that the 'new' artist is an outsider at odds with the philistine society he is observing, and its affirmation that this is a logical and inevitable development which carries with it the blessing of the artistic spirit of all ages, made *Michael Kramer* an impressive curtain-raiser to the twentieth century, an intention surely audible in the grieving father's final words:

Where shall we land? where are we heading? Why do we sometimes exult at the prospect of the unknown? we midgets, lost and forsaken in this immensity? As if we knew the destination.... It won't be an earthly paradise; it won't be the heaven parsons preach about. It won't be the one, and it won't be the other. But what... what *will* it be in the end?

'Before Sunset': the end of an era

The première of *Before Sunset* (*Vor Sonnenuntergang*) on 16 February 1932 at the Deutsches Theater, Berlin, was the last of those glittering Hauptmann first nights which had become such a feature of the German social and artistic calendar since the young revolutionary of 1889 had become Germany's 'greatest living author'.

His acceptance had begun with the enormous box-office success of *The Sunken Bell* in 1896; the University of Oxford had awarded him an honorary doctorate in 1905 and the celebrations and performances which marked his jubilee in 1912 all over the German-speaking world had culminated in the award of that year's Nobel Prize for Literature. With the founding of the Weimar Republic in 1919, the critic of Imperial Germany came into his own; the tubercular and temperamental young man of 1889 had filled out. 'There was a largeness, an almost regal quality about him,' Max Beerbohm observed; 'he looked and behaved as a great man should look and behave.' The comparisons which some people had been drawing between him and Goethe were becoming more appropriate than ever; it was even rumoured that he was thinking of putting himself forward as a candidate for the presidency of Weimar Germany. Sir William Rothenstein, the distinguished artist, met him on holiday in Italy in 1925 and recalled, 'When he strode down, in loud patterned plus-fours, from his villa into the town, hatless, his hair blown back from his high forehead, he always commanded respect.'

Now, in 1932, his latest play was to be directed by the world-famous Max Reinhardt, who had already directed a number of Hauptmann productions; but it was to be for the last time, for Reinhardt left Germany in 1933. The leading role in the play – that of the ageing businessman and philanthropist Matthias Clausen – was taken by Werner Krauss, one of the most distinguished actors of his generation, with Helene Thimig, another great name of the German theatre, as the young kindergarten teacher with whom he falls in love. In Miles Malleson's English version at the Shaftesbury Theatre, London, in 1933, the role was taken by Peggy Ashcroft, with Krauss again in the lead.

Hauptmann was the same age as his hero. His seventieth birthday was being celebrated, as Clausen's is as the play opens. In the autumn of 1932, 176 productions of his plays were mounted in Germany alone. His triumphant visit to the United States earlier that year had projected his international image as the cultural ambassador of a democratic Germany. The play which he contributed to his own celebrations (which happened to coincide with the centenary of Goethe's death) gave the superficial impression of being entertainment in the grand manner of much contemporary drama. The curtain rises on a spacious and well-appointed room; it is a hot summer's day and the sound of a jazz band is floating up from the garden where a party is in progress: under the most auspicious circumstances a family reunion is taking place to celebrate the seventieth birthday of the town's most illustrious citizen, Matthias Clausen, the respected and influential chairman of the board of his family firm. But, as in later examples of the 'family reunion' genre, such as T. S. Eliot's *The Family Reunion* (1939) and J. B. Priestley's *Time and the Conways* (1937), present happiness and optimism are shot through with unwelcome echoes of the past and ominous portents of the future; indeed, Hauptmann's play turns into something of a comedy of menace, too, with moments that anticipate Pinter's *The Birthday Party* (1958) and hark back to his own early drama of family catastrophe, *The Reconciliation* of 1890.

The trouble, at least ostensibly, is caused by Herr Clausen's growing infatuation with a young kindergarten teacher, Inken Peters, which arouses the disapproval and escalating hostility of his whole family. They see it not simply as an embarrassingly silly symptom of the old man's dotage, but as a threat to everything they hold most dear – that is, their late mother's memory or, rather, the fortune they confidently hope to inherit. Their efforts to counter the old man's wishes lead to an unholy alliance between his eldest son, an austere academic, and his son-in-law, a *parvenu* who occupies a junior position in Herr Clausen's firm. The sunny atmosphere of the opening scene gradually clouds over until, towards the end of the play, Clausen's attempt to marry Inken, leave Germany and take up residence in Switzerland is thwarted by his children's last-ditch ploy to have him certified insane so that he forfeits his right to administer his own affairs and funds without their approval and authority.

The central scene of the play, in which Herr Clausen leads Fräulein Peters in to dinner at the family home, only to discover that no place has been set for her, is justly famous, for here, out of an apparently trivial middle-class situation, Hauptmann generates a storm of more than just domestic proportions in which reminiscences of King Lear, dispossessed and at his children's mercy, merge with a bitterly up-to-date struggle between the older man and Klamroth, his pushing son-in-law. Klamroth argues that love and kindness are neither here nor there; resolute leadership is all that matters; one cannot pledge oneself to serve on board a sinking ship; the hands of the clock cannot be put back. Listening to these words, Clausen senses that his time is running out and realises that he is doomed, as is all he stands for; from now on his sole objective is to play for time and hold the inevitable at bay for as long as he possibly can. The original five-act version ends with his suicide; in the later four-act version, which most producers now prefer, a heart attack serves much the same purpose: the tragic victim goes under.

On the day following the première, a review appeared in the *Völkischer Beobachter*, the newspaper of the German National Socialist Workers' Party, which made it clear that some observers at least had understood the drift of the play. The critic described it as 'the sunset of an era' and as 'the end of the liberal theatre in Germany'. Ten days later Adolf Hitler, an Austrian by birth, formally took on German nationality, and in the election later that year his party, supported by a growing number of voters who shared the views and attitudes put forward by Klamroth, became the largest single political grouping in the Reichstag. Between these two events, the German Chancellor, Brüning, was brought down by a collusion of interests which reflected the increasingly unstable state of the nation. Hauptmann, fêted and famous, viewed these ominous developments with apprehension and despondency, like a prophet watching his worst prophecies come true. 'The best is condemned to impotence,' he wrote. 'If Goethe were alive today, we could do with him to lead us.' There was an added irony in the fact that he had modelled his tragic hero, Clausen, on a friend of his, Max Pinkus, who, like Clausen, was a great admirer of Goethe and also a wealthy industrialist and philanthropist whose family had almost driven him to suicide when he had attempted to remarry. By 1934 Pinkus too was dead. Hauptmann and his wife found that they were the only non-Jews to attend his funeral.

Hauptmann's contribution to the Goethe centenary year was a finely constructed work, noble in intention and realistic in manner. Its topicality makes it a fascinating period piece in which Hauptmann's ability to people his stage with characters who embody whole sectors of society and their problems enabled him to create a first-hand response to a crucial turning-point in modern German history. Though the play is often overlooked by writers on the period, it has a great deal to tell us about the atmosphere in Germany in the months immediately preceding the Nazi seizure of power: with consummate ease (one wonders whether it was deliberate or not) Hauptmann brought together a group of characters who, without realising it, represent the various outlooks and vested interests which in 1932 found themselves having to respond to the imminent political upheaval: the up-and-coming industrialist with a chip on his shoulder, the scholarly German academic, the arrogant daughter of a 1914–18 general, with her narrow patriotism born of defeat, the stay-at-home middle-class woman anxious not to have to think about it all, and the hero himself, a man of deep culture steeped in the humanist ideals of Germany's classical writers and thinkers – they all ring amazingly true and may well turn out to be the most vivid reminders to later audiences of what is no longer remembered at first hand.

Present-day productions of *Before Sunset* demonstrate that it also works in other ways and on other levels. A notable Swiss production at the Berne municipal theatre in 1977 deliberately played down the implicit allusions to Weimar Germany in 1932 and instead emphasised the desperate nature of Herr Clausen's bid for a new lease of life. By concentrating on the symptoms of senility Clausen develops as the play progresses, and the steps taken by his family to cope with a genuine problem, it brought out the power and pathos of the play as a study of the painful process of growing old. As Clausen says, 'You simply cannot imagine what a deep abyss a life of seventy years is: it makes one giddy to look down into it.' Hauptmann was of course speaking from the heart: he was only too aware that he had reached the age of three-score years and ten, the limit traditionally set to human life, and that the rest was a bonus, or rather, when viewed from 1932, a future heavy with dark and forbidding menace. Looking back over his richly productive life, he wryly commented, 'My era began with the creation of Bismarck's Germany in 1870 and ended with the burning of the Reichstag.' The fire which destroyed the Parliament building in Berlin took place in February 1933, exactly a year after the opening night of *Before Sunset*. From that moment on, his era was indeed over, as the National Socialist drama critic had pointed out. 'Silence is the greatest art,' Hauptmann reminded himself. But how does a great writer remain silent?

Hauptmann did not remain silent. His last years were spent writing a sequence of plays on the Greek myth of the sacrifice of Iphigenia (1940–4) which most critics have dismissed as irrelevant, which did not speak out, but which had plenty to say to those who had ears to hear. His private view of the human condition and his apprehensions about the future had already found expression in a number of works in which normal everyday reality gives way to a blacker vision shot through and even enhanced by occasional shafts of light. *The Black Mask* (*Die schwarze Maske*) is a case in point: this one-act play – a genre unusual for Hauptmann – was written in 1929, and has regained interest now that it has been 'salvaged' as the basis for a major stage work by the leading contemporary Polish composer, Penderecki, premièred at the Salzburg Festival in 1986.

The action is set in 1662, which was also a post-war period in Germany (the Thirty Years War had ended in 1648): by 1662 things should have got better, even back to normal. But have they? As a group of widely disparate people gather for dinner at the home of the wealthy burgomaster Schuller, a blizzard blows outside, and his opulent dining-room is plunged into unnatural midday darkness. What ensues is a tautly constructed drama during which a generous-spirited man's attempt to preserve peace and harmony is vitiated by the remorseless and destructive workings of human guilt – guilt which is in some cases conscious but, what is worse, is sometimes subconscious too. Eat, drink and be merry is the order of the day; as the characters dine, carnival revellers cavort in the wintry streets outside. But already the first rats have been sighted, sure bearers of the black death, bubonic plague. Are members of the dinner party already infected? Is the burgomaster's beautiful young wife dying upstairs? Was the front door left open by mistake to admit the gaunt figure of a reveller dressed up as Death? Who is the handsome negro whose hand leaves an ominous black mark on the gleaming white starched damask tablecloth?

A German burgomaster, a man of authority respected by his fellow citizens and confident in his probity and prosperity, yet threatened by forces that will ultimately bring him down: the theme was one which Hauptmann had already treated in one of his bleakest, most pessimistic plays, *Magnus Garbe*. Set in the sixteenth century, which in Germany was a period of religious upheaval and of social and political turmoil, it was actually written during the First World War, but he withheld it from publication until the middle of the Second, by which point in modern German history, he thought, humanity had reached a level low enough to be able to take it and, perhaps, understand what he was getting at. Its first performance did not take place until 1956, the same year as Dürrenmatt's *The Visit* (*Der Besuch der alten Dame*), which, being the most re-markable German-language play of its time, naturally over-shadowed it. Yet Hauptmann's play, the black product of two world wars, has similarities with Dürrenmatt's grisly political and moral allegory of post-war Switzerland. It charts the hounding and destruction of Burgomaster Garbe and his beautiful wife Felicia, a serene, contented, cultured couple who are the products of late-medieval ease and prosperity, but who become the unwitting and innocent victims of mounting prejudice and hostility when the community they lead and love is taken over by the Inquisition in the aftermath of the Reformation.

Hauptmann's slow, deliberate, painfully sustained depiction of the growth of violence and lawlessness in a hitherto ordered and contented community is impressive. Smoke clouds are seen rising in the distance and rabid dogs roam the streets as, indoors, the beautiful Felicia sits to a Flemish portrait painter. All is well; the birth of her baby confidently expected. They converse in muted, intimate tones; the sky darkens, storm clouds gather, the wind rises; Felicia is all serene composure when, suddenly, a window shatters. That first traumatic sound, the smashing of glass: no other play captures so well the terror so many people experienced between 1914 and 1942, and its neglect by the modern theatre is all the more difficult to explain. Of course the play is ostensibly set in the past and may give the superficial impression of being nothing more than old-fashioned costume drama; but Hauptmann had given sufficient proof that his ability to dramatise contemporary society was second to none, and his artistic decision to set this particular existential drama in another time and place should be seen for what it was – an attempt to distance himself from contemporary events so as to convey their true significance with total detachment and explicit clarity in defiance of the constraints of current ideology and political censorship. It was what Sartre was doing with *The Flies* (*Les Mouches*) in occupied France in 1942.

Darker still, but with many points in common with *The Black Mask* and *Magnus Garbe*, Hauptmann's *Darknesses* (*Die Finsternisse*) is a short drama composed in 1937 in memory of his Jewish friend Max Pinkus. First performed on the BBC Third Programme in 1947, it is an imaginary reconstruction of the funeral supper held in honour of the man who in many respects provided the model for Matthias Clausen and the other dominant figures in Hauptmann's later works, who, though men of substance, cultured, kindly and public-spirited, prove to be unequal to the challenges with which they are ineluctably confronted. As the Old Testament prophet Elijah, the 'beloved disciple' John and Ahasuerus the wandering Jew join the supper party in the villa of the deceased industrialist in a Silesian town in 1934, the vaster dimensions of topical events take on immediate shape, bringing home the deep personal significance which this eternally tragic theme possessed for Hauptmann towards the end of his life. Theatre-goers, however, have scarcely yet had the chance to appreciate the ways in which the major German dramatist of the first half of the twentieth century gave artistic form to the catastrophe which engulfed him and his generation.

In May 1945 the Red Army occupied Silesia. The many admirers of his working-class dramas such as *The Weavers* urged him to move to the Russian zone of Berlin, but Hauptmann, now aged over eighty, obstinately refused to be dislodged from his birthplace along with the millions of German-speakers who were being expelled from what was now Polish territory. He died on 6 June 1946, and was buried on an island in the Baltic where he had spent many a happy holiday.

2
Frank Wedekind

Wedekind on Theatre

Actors are always trying to find a special style for me. But that is not what I want, damn it! You see, I should be played quite straightforwardly. They should perform me just as they perform the classics. What my plays cannot stand is a naturalistic approach, with hands in pockets and the words sloppily mumbled so that nobody can catch them. And please spare me your psychological subtleties: there is no such thing as 'psychological' style – the psychological dimension goes without saying and will emerge of its own accord if my characters are presented consistently. Their psychology is my business, it is not the business of my characters, still less of the actors playing them. I want to be performed as the classics used to be performed at the Burgtheater in Vienna, i.e. with maximum care given to bringing out the individuality of each character, and with the closest, exactest attention to the words. Even pathos doesn't scare me provided my speeches are heard and each word is distinctly and separately articulated so as to make sense. The actor who plays Macbeth or Othello ought also

to be able to play my Marquis von Keith, and I should like to
see my Schigolch being played by the same actor who usually
takes the parts of King Lear and Shylock. My Lulu is an
ingénue, and should only be played by the young lady who
normally plays Ophelia and Gretchen in Goethe's *Faust*.

(Reported by Arthur Kahane, 1928)

Schnitzler on Wedekind

Have been reading some more Wedekind recently. To think that
there are people who take it seriously as art! He writes essays
of moderate profundity in the form of dialogues, and in language
which is certainly very individual but so mannered as to lose
all vitality. They are autobiographical sketches by a highly
original but inflexible and limited entertainer who was once a
serious writer.   (Diary entry, 1918)

Hauptmann on Wedekind

He beats me when it comes to relentless truthfulness.

(Autobiography, 1937, book II, ch. 41)

Introduction

Wedekind wrote plays about sex. To this he owes his reputation.
But he also used the stage to expose the conventional hypocrisies
of society and show the tragi-comic consequences of the images
people project or which the world imposes on them.

Benjamin Franklin Wedekind was conceived in the United
States, born in Germany and brought up in Switzerland. His
birth took place in Hanover in 1864, just two years before it
was incorporated into Bismarck's Prussia by force of arms: he
was to be the relentless critic of the Prussian-dominated German
Empire all his life, dying, ironically, just before its defeat in
1918. He did not live to see the advent of the Weimar Republic,
whose artistic tone he had done so much to prepare. Like

Schnitzler, he was a doctor's son, and both his parents had strongly-held progressive liberal views. They had met in San Francisco, where Wedekind's mother, orphaned and already divorced, was earning her living in music-hall. Dr Wedekind and his young wife returned to Germany, but in 1871 the founding of the Second German Empire made them take up residence in the more congenial climate of German-speaking Switzerland, where Frank was educated. He went to Munich in 1884 to study law, and it was there that he emerged as a writer.

Like Berlin and Vienna, Munich was the centre of lively cultural activity in the nineteenth century, and, like Berlin, it was becoming a focus of the new Naturalist movement, with whose leading lights Wedekind was soon associated. The Munich Naturalists favoured prose fiction and admired Zola, but Wedekind knew from the start that he was a born dramatist. His first play, *The Fast Painter, or Art and Mammon* (*Der Schnellmaler oder Kunst und Mammon*) dates from 1886, was published in 1889, and was first performed in 1916; its title at once indicates Wedekind's reluctance to comply in all seriousness with the Naturalist doctrine of realism in the theatre. His second play, a comedy called *Children and Fools* (*Kinder und Narren*, 1891), later reworked as *The Young World* (*Die junge Welt*, 1897) is a satirical send-up of the Naturalist writers, with some female emancipation thrown in for good measure, and was written partly in retaliation for Hauptmann's portrayal of domestic squabbles in Wedekind's temperamental family in *The Reconciliation*. Wedekind's most productive creative phase was about to begin. In 1891 he completed *Spring Awakening* (*Frühlings Erwachen*), which in 1895 was followed by the first version or instalment of his 'monster tragedy' charting the career of Lulu.

Journalism, love affairs (including one with Strindberg's ex-wife, Frida Uhl), exile in Paris, imprisonment in Germany on a charge of *lèse-majesté*, work as an actor, producer and cabaret entertainer in Munich, legal complications over the second part of the Lulu drama, and marriage to Tilly Newes, the actress who created the role of Lulu in Vienna – all these seemed to be the stages in Wedekind's gradual ascent to general artistic acceptability, culminating in the celebrations which marked his fiftieth birthday in 1914, when plays of his were put on in many German-speaking theatres. But whereas both Schnitzler and Hauptmann had been able to enjoy their greatest artistic triumphs in times of peace and prosperity, Wedekind's real breakthrough occurred on the eve of the First World War.

Germany had a tradition of sharply observant theatrical satire dating back to the days of the Reformation, when the folly, gullibility and superstition of humanity were publicly caricatured and ridiculed. Such plays always contained a good measure of slapstick: they painted in broad strokes, hit hard, and used words economically and for effect rather than to create a semblance of real life on stage. Wedekind, 400 years later, belongs in that tradition and was himself largely responsible for its modern revival in Germany. He was the heir, too, of the passionate but disjointed energy of the young *Sturm and Drang* writers of the 1770s, and shares their furious contempt for respectability and their impatience with complacency in all its forms. The theatrical background of Wedekind's drama is unique to Germany, however, and this accounts for the difficulties which actors, producers and audiences in other countries tend to have when trying to come to terms with his plays. Seen from outside the orbit of German theatrical culture, Wedekind appears startlingly modern and iconoclastically original; within it, he can be appreciated as a vital link in a tradition going back to Hans Sachs (1494–1576), and which was handed on to him by Georg Büchner (1813–37), the author of *Woyzeck*. He in turn handed it on to Brecht and Dürrenmatt.

Wedekind's work can be inconsistent and sound flat. But at its best it provides the kind of experiences we have come to regard in the later twentieth century as typically theatrical. Realism of the cinematographic kind meant nothing to him: his plays are essays in practical theatre. They smell of greasepaint and have a look of fancy-dress; they call for teamwork as well as individual commitment. Theatre workshops seem their proper habitat, rather than the great houses where flawless perfection is the aim. Yet, paradoxically, the 'Wedekind style' is not easy for inexperienced actors or producers to achieve, which may be a reason why he has never gained anything like the popularity of his admirer, Brecht. It has been known for a long time that Wedekind is a very fine playwright, but a Wedekind performance which actually works is still a rare treat.

'Spring Awakening'

Spring Awakening (*Frühlings Erwachen*) earned Wedekind his notoriety as a provocatively controversial playwright. It was written during the winter of 1890–1 in Munich after his return from a short visit to Berlin, where he had been exposed to the views and personalities of some of the leading Naturalist writers in the German capital, and it has more in common with their approach than any of his later plays. It also demonstrates his early admiration for Georg Büchner, whose works he and Hauptmann had been doing something to resuscitate; indeed *Spring Awakening* has been described as the only true successor to Büchner's *Woyzeck* before the inter-war period, when both writers became a major influence on young German playwrights. As Wedekind openly admitted, 'Without *Woyzeck*, my first drama, *Spring Awakening*, would never have come into being'.

Wedekind paid for its publication out of his own purse in 1891, but it remained quite unknown to the general public until its première at the Berlin Kammerspiele, a newly-opened experimental theatre, on 20 November 1906 in a production by Max Reinhardt. His production, with its masterly use of the most up-to-date staging-techniques (revolving stage, no 'realistic' sets, gauzes) set a precedent for later productions of a work soon regarded in the German-speaking countries as the spearhead of a new concept of drama. Moreover it ran for 351 performances, proving that the new and controversial could go down well with an audience, such as the one in Berlin, which was relatively receptive to new ideas (though the text had had to be toned down somewhat to satisfy the censor). Max Reinhardt's backing was to prove important for Wedekind's career as a playwright. Though Reinhardt personally produced only *Spring Awakening* (in 1906, and again in 1918 and 1925), the theatres he controlled provided Wedekind with a valuable springboard. *Spring Awakening*, for instance, had been regarded as controversial since its publication in 1891, but when Reinhardt's company started to take it on tour from 1907 onwards, its impact on theatre audiences grew rapidly; indeed, no other German play this century has achieved such high production and performance figures. It is perhaps significant, however, that since the 1950s these have tended to to tail off; this may well be the result of the increasing permissiveness of the 1960s. If so, this is something of a vindication of Wedekind's reforming purpose in writing the play. Even as early as 1929 attempts were being made in Germany to update it in order to save it from the ridicule of a more knowing generation; but Wedekind would have relished the notoriety it attracted when it was given two performances by the English Stage Society at the Royal Court Theatre, London, in 1963, in a version by Tom Osborn, only to be rejected by the National Theatre two years later (the National eventually staged the play in 1974, in a version by Edward Bond).

Why all the controversy? Basing his drama on his own boyhood experiences (he said himself that almost every scene corresponded to real events), Wedekind created the unthinkable – a play about sex, or, rather, about the awakening of three sensitive young teenagers to their own sexuality and to the emotional demands it rouses in them. By tracing the phenomenon of sexuality back to its early stirrings during adolescence, Wedekind's play broke a powerful taboo and at the same time pointed forward to what was to become an often obsessive theme in twentieth-century literature; for with *Spring Awakening* the adolescent came of age as a figure of independent literary and dramatic importance, whose existence and experiences midway between the nursery and the drawing-room were intrinsically interesting and valid in their own right.

Caught between the semi-sentimentalised innocence of the late Victorian image of childhood and the stark though as yet only dimly sensed realities of the stuffy world inhabited by their elders and so-called betters, Wedekind's teenagers experience joys and sufferings appropriate to the phase they are passing through, but none the less real, intense and sometimes cruel for all that. Hampered by the evasiveness of their parents and teachers, and unable to accept their conventional and hollow guidance, though not yet fully able to contradict it, Wendla, Moritz and Melchior escape from their emotional confusion into worlds of intensely real make-believe. Two of them prove incapable of emerging from this adolescent phase. Wendla, pregnant without realising it, dies prematurely, the victim of her respectable middle-class mother's misguided attempt to remove potential embarrassment by illegal pseudo-medical means, all for the sake of appearances, while Moritz opts out of his problems at home, at school and in himself by committing suicide. Will Melchior survive to grow up into a normal balanced adult? There is hope for him at the end of the play, when a masked gentleman unexpectedly appears and coaxes him away from the graveyard where his two young friends are buried, promising to open up the whole wide world to him.

The part of the masked gentleman was one which Wedekind,

in top hat and frock coat, very much liked to act himself, and it is significant that the play is actually dedicated to this novel Edwardian reincarnation of the traditional *deus ex machina*. When seen in terms of its *dénouement*, the play is clearly a plea by Wedekind to his potential audiences to accept the facts of life openly and frankly, and to assert themselves by stepping out into the future without any false illusions. Adolescence is so short-lived; vivid and searing though its experiences are, they should coincide with a growing awareness that it is time to grow up. The freedom and independence of maturity cannot be fully achieved, however, if the natural need for knowledge about the facts of life is repressed or rejected. Wendla and her mother try to suppress it, and Moritz, too, cannot face up to it. Neither Wendla nor Moritz will ever grow up to reach maturity, and that, in Wedekind's view, is their tragedy. The theme of his provocative, often shocking, study of adolescence thus unexpectedly turns out to have something in common with *Peter Pan*, J. M. Barrie's light-hearted dramatic fantasy of 1904, subtitled 'The boy who wouldn't grow up'.

Spring Awakening is not an easy play to pin down, because in it Wedekind combine elements of fantasy and the grotesque with a display of uncompromising social verisimilitude in what might be termed the Berlin manner. The final scene provides a good example. It is a bright November night. On the bushes and trees the desiccated foliage rattles. Torn clouds scud past the moon. Thus the stage-directions as Melchior climbs the churchyard wall and jumps down inside. The macabre atmosphere is in sharp contrast to that of some of the other scenes, such as the garden of Wendla Bergmann's home in Act II scene vi, as she wanders about in the glow of the morning sunshine, and this deliberate contrast is further reinforced when Moritz Stiefel comes stomping over the graves carrying his head beneath his arm. This grotesque episode comes far closer to the horrors of Victorian melodrama than to the realism of the

Naturalist writers, if it is taken literally, but what the audience sees is really a figment of Melchior's overheated imagination, and Wedekind is using what amounts to a form of alienation effect in order to deflect the attention of his spectators away from the superficial externals of realism to the inner realities of his character's mind. Up to a point this is similar to Hauptmann's dramatic exploration of the fantasy world of a dying girl in his 'dream play' *Hannele* (1893). Yet the sudden intervention of the masked gentleman and his altercation with Moritz's headless ghost brings out the quasi-allegorical dimension of the drama, and shows that even in this early play Wedekind was intent on establishing a different rapport between stage and audience by using his characters to represent points of view rather than simply to present them. The schoolteachers who convene beneath the enlightened portraits of Rousseau and Pestalozzi at the beginning of Act III to discuss the problems raised by Melchior's 'obscenities' are further examples of Wedekind's fondness for satirical comedy; their graphic but quite unrealistic names suggest that the action of the play at this point is being seen partly through the eyes of their pupils, who would naturally delight in apt nicknames such as Wedekind gives them.

When he wants to, Wedekind is perfectly capable of handling the Naturalistic mode, with its insistence on idiomatic dialogue and the interaction of characters drawn from life. His ability in this respect is often not fully exploited in his later plays, because of the preference he increasingly displayed for a German equivalent of Shavian abstraction by means of which he could propagate his own, often conflicting views. The realist Wedekind is at his finest in the scene (II.ii) in which Frau Bergmann tells her daughter Wendla that she has become an 'auntie' for the third time, an announcement which leads via the proverbial stork to Frau Bergmann's bungled attempts to answer yet not answer her daughter's perfectly natural questions.

The facts of life (or at least their verbal expression!) are too much for the good lady. In desperation she has recourse to the vague notion of 'married love': love is thus revealed to be a euphemism for sex, with the further paradoxical implication that it would be a very pleasant alternative to it, at least from Frau Bergmann's point of view, and the chaster, the better. Wendla, meanwhile, should continue to remain young enough to prefer chocolates and cake! This scene is Wedekind's most memorable achievement in the realistic mode. Shortly afterwards, Wendla finds Melchior in a hayloft as a storm is blowing up outside. What her mother had so squeamishly concealed, young Melchior, who thinks he knows it all, reveals. As Wendla's initiation proceeds, the affinities to Schnitzler's *Round Dance* are close, though Wedekind's irony is more obvious, and serves more clearly to emphasise his own attitude:

WENDLA. Don't kiss me, Melchior! – stop kissing me.
MELCHIOR. Your heart – I can hear it beating.
WENDLA. Kissing means you love someone. Stop it! Don't!
MELCHIOR. Believe me, there's no such thing as love. It's all selfishness, all egoism. I don't love you any more than you love me.
WENDLA. Stop it! Don't, Melchior!
MELCHIOR. ...Wendla!
WENDLA. Oh, Melchior!...Don't...please....

Her pleas are in vain. Melchior, true to type as a healthy young male, has already told his friend Moritz that he does not want anything he does not have to fight to get, a view which his more introverted friend finds repugnant. But his talk of egoism, though plainly dictated by his need to reassure Wendla, who seems afraid of 'love', also expresses his own juvenile philosophy: selfishness seems to account for most of the human behaviour he sees around him, as well as for his own. It is also the sound basis for survival and, ultimately, for liberation. As the masked gentleman tells him right at the end, morality, the morality of the real adult world, is the product of two imaginary quantities, *sollen* and *wollen*, what one ought to do and what one wants to do. Wedekind's 'immoral' play was the work of a moralist in disguise.

Spring Awakening is often interpreted as a tragedy of natural healthy adolescence repressed and destroyed by social convention; but this is an oversimplified view. Seen in the context of Wedekind's other plays, it is the 'adolescent' prelude to a lifelong exploration and dramatisation of the forces and impulses which shape the lives of human beings and dictate their interactions and relations with each other. To contemporaries, however, it was first and foremost a daring dramatic expression of things that were on people's minds. Some producers saw it as a wistful, sometimes angry, elegy on the transience of childhood, while others presented it as a scathing exposure of hypocritical taboos. Wedekind had certainly broken a conspiracy of silence. His pioneering venture was promptly followed by a spate of works on similar subjects, including Max Halbe's play *Youth* (*Jugend*, 1893), one of the German theatre's greatest box-office successes during the 'naughty nineties'. But it is Wedekind's play that has survived. The composer Gustav Mahler was right to describe it as 'powerful, immensely talented, and full of poetry'.

The Lulu plays

At the end of *Spring Awakening* the masked gentleman leads young Melchior off into the wider world. This world, where many things are forbidden but where anything can happen, is the setting for the Lulu plays, Wedekind's masterpiece.

Their composition, stage-history and interpretation are very problematic. Wedekind began work on his new project in 1892, and a version of the first play appeared in 1895 under the title *Der Erdgeist* (*The Earth Spirit*). His original intention had been to write one gigantic five-act Lulu drama (he liked to call it his 'monster tragedy'), but the 1895 text consists only of Acts I, II and IV of the original scheme, with a new Act III. This meant that the last two acts of the original turned into a more or less self-contained sequel which was published in 1902 under the title *Die Büchse der Pandora* (*Pandora's Box*) with an additional first act by way of exposition. The story does not end there.

Constant alterations, in part forced on him by the constrictions of official censorship, and in part by his own changing ideas and his first-hand experience gained in performance, resulted in a number of amended versions, until in 1913 the collected edition of Wedekind's works finally made a reliable reading-text available. The theatres tended to want something rather different, however: what they wanted above all was a play which could be performed in one evening, not two. The result was that Wedekind (and others) made a variety of stage adaptations: his own 1913 *Lulu* and that by his daughter Kadidja in 1950 are the most important. In Germany these compressed stage adaptations have never really caught on; instead the two Lulu plays have tended to go their separate ways.

Earth Spirit was first performed in 1898 in Leipzig and taken on tour to other cities, including Munich, by a company calling itself the Ibsen-Theater, with Wedekind himself in the role of Dr Schön; a Berlin production followed at Max Reinhardt's Kleines Theater in 1902 with the glamorous Gertrud Eysoldt in the role of Lulu. *Earth Spirit* remains one of Wedekind's most successful plays, second only to *Spring Awakening* in number of performances and to *The Tenor* (*Der Kammersänger*) in number of productions on the German stage, though from the end of the First World War and on through the 1920s its sequel, *Pandora's Box*, exerted greater appeal.

Pandora's Box was first seen in closed performances in Nuremberg (1904) and in Vienna (1905) in a production staged by the Austrian satirical writer Karl Kraus, with Tilly Newes as Lulu and Wedekind as Jack the Ripper. Occasional open performances began to take place from 1911, and, when these were officially permitted in 1918, the play became a *succès de scandale* and thus a box-office success. The 1920s image of Berlin owes much to it. In Britain acceptance of the Lulu plays came much more slowly and has been sporadic. The tendency has been to stage them in compressed adaptations which give a slicker, brasher impression: examples are Peter Barnes's 1970 version and Leon Rubin's two-act adaptation of Peter Tegel's translation, which won applause and critical acclaim at the Palace Theatre, Watford, in 1985.

The Lulu plays have excited strident reactions especially in the English-speaking world, because they exemplify a conception of drama that is very un-English. Their uninhibited view of what goes on behind the social façade may provide a *frisson* of embarrassed delight, but the view persists that such things may happen in Berlin and Vienna, but they do not happen here: even Wedekind's authentic Jack the Ripper cannot overcome this culture gap. The fact remains that Wedekind intended the two plays to be seen as dramas drawn from life – not literally, in the 'photographic' way associated with the Naturalist movement, but in such a way that, if audiences were really honest with themselves, they would recognise Lulu's world as a valid dimension of their own as seen through the eyes of a creative writer with a strong sense of his own personal viewpoint and with a highly developed sense of stagecraft. Wedekind's distribution of light and shade, like the emphasis – some might call it overemphasis – he places on some episodes and themes and his discretion or indeed indifference regarding others, create a skilfully co-ordinated sequence of dramatic pictures portraying a world which has now largely vanished.

1a. Gerhart Hauptmann, c. 1895

1b. Frank Wedekind, c. 1905.

1c. Arthur Schnitzler, c. 1910.

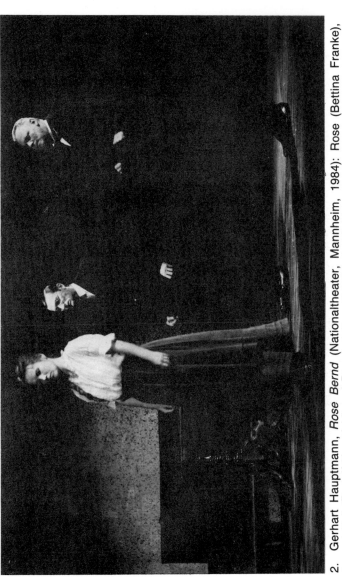

2. Gerhart Hauptmann, *Rose Bernd* (Nationaltheater, Mannheim, 1984): Rose (Bettina Franke), August Keil (Rudolf Kowalski) and Rose's father (Adolf Laimböck).

3. Gerhart Hauptmann, *Rose Bernd* (Nationaltheater, Mannheim, 1984): Streckmann (Roland Bayer) attacking Keil (Rudolf Kowalski) as Rose's father (Adolf Laimböck) looks on.

4. Frank Wedekind, *Lulu* (Komödie, Basle, 1985): Lulu (Bettina Kupfer) and the painter Schwarz (Roberto Bargellini).

5. Frank Wedekind, *Der Marquis von Keith* (Burgtheater, Vienna, 1982): the Marquis (Frank Hoffmann) with Countess Werdenfels, alias Anna Huber (Sonja Sutter).

6. Arthur Schnitzler, *Liebelei*, in Tom Stoppard's adaptation *Dalliance* (National Theatre, London, 1986): Mitzi (Sally Dexter) and Theodore (Tim Curry) have supper with Christine (Brenda Blethyn) and Fritz (Stephen Moore).

7. Arthur Schnitzler, *Reigen* (*The Round Dance*) (Akademietheater, Vienna, 1983): the Count (Peter Wolfsberger) and the Actress (Annemarie Düringer).

8. Arthur Schnitzler, *Reigen* (*The Round Dance*) (Komödie, Basle, 1981): the Husband (Werner Prinz) makes overtures to the Sweet Young Thing (Babett Arens).

That world can be identified quite explicitly from the text; indeed, it is important to get it into focus right from the start. Otherwise interpretations can easily get out of hand and forfeit Wedekind's unobtrusive yet authentic grasp of reality.

The action of the two Lulu plays takes place between 1870 (news of the Paris Commune breaks in Act II of *Earth Spirit*) and 1888–9, when Jack the Ripper was perpetrating his spine-chilling murders in London: Lulu comes to a sticky end as one of his many victims. Though Wedekind generally avoids topical allusions to Germany, it is clear that Lulu's career coincides with the reign of Wilhelm I and the Chancellorship of Bismarck. We first meet her during the economic boom, the so-called *Gründerzeit*, which followed the Franco-Prussian War and created a self-confident new plutocracy in Germany. Capitalism began to dominate public life at this period and to penetrate the public mind at all levels of society; men worked hard to acquire wealth and to improve their social station, and were not afraid to show off their success. The type is caught to perfection, yet humanised with individual traits, in Dr Schön, the dominant male character in *Earth Spirit*. Dr Schön is the proprietor and editor of a newspaper, and the mastermind behind a rapidly expanding press and business empire, a man who can afford the risk and luxury of having the lovely Lulu as his mistress.

The period was one when successful artists were not only the social equals of those who employed their services as portrait painters, but also able to make fortunes never dreamt of before. There is therefore nothing incongruous in the easy relationship between Dr Schön and Lulu's second husband, the artist Schwarz, nor in the deal struck between them after the sudden death of Lulu's first husband, Dr Goll. 'You married half a million,' Schön reminds Schwarz three times in the chilling scene (II.iv) during which he remorselessly destroys the illusions under which, true to German Romantic type, the 'other-worldly' artist has been living. Germany had established itself as a major cultural nation during the eighteenth and nineteenth centuries, and the increasingly affluent German middle class believed by the 1870s that it possessed a monopoly of culture (the theme recurs in Wedekind's later play *The Marquis von Keith*). They enjoyed their sometimes misplaced patronage of the arts, and it was important to their self-esteem to appear cultured and well-read.

It was at this time that the characteristically German forms of address, such as 'Herr Doktor' (indicative of a postgraduate academic education), were becoming accepted as social assets, along with their feminine forms, such as 'Frau Doktor', which applied to the wives of men with postgraduate degrees. When the play opens, Lulu is the wife of a well-to-do physician called Dr Goll; in Act II scene ii, when she first appears, Dr Schön kisses her hand as befits a lady and addresses her as 'Frau Medizinalrat', indicating that she is the consort of a 'medical counsellor', i.e. a doctor. Some minutes later, the artist Schwarz betrays his humbler origins by going one further and addressing Lulu as 'Frau Obermedizinalrat': the addition of that extra 'Ober' is a neat touch, easily overlooked, which betrays acute social observation and a naughty satirical eye. Wedekind's plays are full of such delights. The insistence on titles and forms of address at the start of the play, together with the life-style that goes with them, establishes a social framework for the action and gives Lulu a social status in relation to which her later decline and fall can be measured. Initially, her standing conveys substance and respectability. But the latter is as superficial as the former is recent. Behind his appearance of distinguished sobriety, Dr Goll turns out to be an elderly *roué* to whom Schön has married Lulu in order to ensure himself easy access to her and provide her with a fortune and a foothold in society. In fact, Frau Medizinalrat Goll is none other than the girl he picked up off the streets when she was selling flowers in front of the Alhambra Café, and whom he made something of – or corrupted, depending on one's viewpoint. The similarity of the initial situation to that in Shaw's *Pygmalion* is interesting, but so too is the subsequent divergence between Lulu's relationship to Dr Schön and that of Eliza Doolittle to her mentor, Professor Higgins. Like *Pygmalion*, *Earth Spirit* is a sharply satirical depiction of social attitudes, but the difference in tone between the two plays tells us a lot about the different relationships between playwright and audience in England and Germany before 1914. Wedekind's Lulu plays are as serious in intention as the social plays of Hauptmann and Schnitzler, and their texts are rich in hints and allusions which indicate his powers as an observer of the behaviour and values of his contemporaries. If 'social drama' seems a misnomer to many admirers and modern producers of the play, this is probably the result of Wedekind's preference for self-contained and often meticulously worked-out episodes, rather than for the sustained continuity of action and argument associated with the type of social drama which Ibsen and Hauptmann, and Chekhov too, had perfected. The dissimilarities between the two approaches become even more evident in *Pandora's Box*, where the setting shifts from the late Dr Schön's solid, well-appointed German villa (the scene of the last act of *Earth Spirit*) to an opulent Paris salon reminiscent of the demimonde of *La Dame aux camélias*, La Traviata or indeed of *Du côté de chez Swann*, and then, finally, to a damp and sordid garret in London, three settings which graphically convey the stages in Lulu's progress and downfall.

From start to finish, from Frau Medizinalrat Goll to London prostitute, the arc of Lulu's career is subtly accompanied by the presence of her portrait, to which Schwarz is putting the finishing touches as *Earth Spirit* opens. Lulu's portrait is a fine example of the key function a stage prop can have in a modern drama, and any production blind enough to overlook it misses a vital dimension – the implicit contrast it constantly suggests between then and now. To ignore this dimension is to falsify Wedekind's conception, because it is precisely by such means that he realises it in theatrical terms. When Schwarz first places the portrait on his easel in Act I to the discerning admiration of his patron, Dr Schön, a stage-direction tells us that it depicts '*a lady dressed as a pierrot*'. In Act II (the scene is now the elegant home she shares with Schwarz), it hangs over the mantelpiece in a rich brocade frame; in Act IV (when she is married to Schön) we see it displayed on an ornamental easel and encircled by a reproduction antique gilt frame. The portrait is absent as *Pandora's Box* opens, but is duly restored, all dusty, to its rightful position by Alwa, Schön's son, soon after Lulu's escape from the prison to which she was remanded for her murder of Dr Schön at the end of *Earth Spirit*. In Paris, where Lulu is at the mercy of financial exploitation and feels very insecure, her portrait, now in a thin gold frame, is set into the wall. In the final act, Countess Geschwitz turns up with it, rolled up, in their London garret. Seeing it again, Alwa contrasts it to Lulu's present appearance in words which echo a famous German poem of the Baroque era, Hofmannswaldau's sonnet on the transience of beauty: 'The childlike expression in her eyes is just the same still, in spite of everything she has been through since. But the fresh dew covering her skin, the fragrant breath about her lips, the brilliant light that radiates from her white brow, and the defiant splendour of that youthful flesh on neck and arms....' – to which old Schigolch, who has known her longest, adds the poignant words, 'All gone with the dustcart. But at least she can say, that was once me, whereas the man who gets her today won't have the faintest idea of what things were like when we were young.'

Lulu's portrait relates to her like that of Dorian Gray to him, but in reverse: it remains young while she grows old (Wilde's novel appeared in 1891, and its German translation in 1901). It also links up with the craze for pierrots which swept through all levels of society from the pier pavilion to French *avant-garde* poetry in the 1890s. Naïve, comic, yet also pathetic, the pierrot figure was associated with wordless mime which conveyed its childish joys and sudden despairs; Lulu's portrait as a pierrot enabled Wedekind to remind audiences throughout the drama of her essential vulnerability. She is of course the central figure in both plays and the pivot of the action, but she never says very much, and what she says is hardly memorable. Yet she holds our attention as spectators, just as she holds that of the men in her life, by simply being what she is: how right it was of Schwarz to paint her as a pierrot, with its connotations of pretty doll and puppet. The pierrot image added a visual dimension to the drama which can still appeal, but which was more heavily laden with associations and richer in suggestive power for audiences in Wedekind's own day. For example, a visitor to Berlin, recording his impressions of Mme Orska's interpretation of the role, commented,

> Her Lulu is not a human being made hideous and fascinating with eternal lures. She is a kind of mask, a thin mask, a shell of tinted and whitened silks over a face sucked dry of all but passion and the shrunken charms of decadence. She is a sort of doll, with her long black legs and her pale face thrust out from either end of a pierrot's costume.

Only in Act II of *Earth Spirit* is the portrait absent. Maybe Wedekind had forgotten its sustained symbolism when he added this act to his original 'monster tragedy' in order to publish its first half as a self-contained drama. But its absence is more likely to be deliberate, for here, where Schön is trying to promote Lulu as a star on the professional stage, we feel that her pretty costumes are a disguise which does not really suit her. Nothing comes of the artistic career on which her patron tries to launch her; her true nature finds expression in other ways. Wedekind's chief claim to fame in dramatising her story is that he gave tangible form to one of the twentieth century's potent myths, the woman sex-symbol in an amoral world; the myth was to take on reality eighty years later in the life and legend of Marilyn Monroe, who had much in common with Wedekind's heroine, though on an even larger, more glamorous transatlantic scale.

The portrait not only provides effective contrast to Lulu's changing situation from act to act; its frames and settings also function as visual correlatives to the ways in which she is treated by the men who take her up, and to the differing images they have of her. It is surrounded by artistic extravagance by Schwarz, the successful society painter; by reproduction gilt by Dr Schön, the prosperous self-made man. After Lulu has killed him, been convicted of his murder, and been rescued from prison by Countess Geschwitz, it is set into the wall of a luxury apartment, like a safe: Lulu has become little more than a lucrative commodity for others to deal in. Her chains may be golden ones, but they restrict her freedom all the same, as she bitterly recognises when the repulsive white-slave dealer Casti-Piani offers her the stark choice between being an ex-convict or a courtesan, and proposes to negotiate a career for her in an exclusive Cairo brothel. By the end, in London, when she is struggling to survive and about to meet her bloody fate at the hands of Jack the Ripper, her image is being lovingly preserved, rolled up, by her devoted friend the Countess; the only other people still around to admire it are the mysterious Schigolch, her so-called father, and Dr Schön's son Alwa, a writer whose words at various points in the drama show his close affinity with Wedekind himself. For example, in Act III scene iii of *Earth Spirit* he muses on Lulu's potential as the protagonist of a drama – but in how many acts? he wonders: while in Act III of *Pandora's Box* he looks back over the various phases of her life and echoes Congreve with his comment 'That's the way of the world'.

To all the men in her life (except perhaps Schigolch and Alwa) Lulu is the embodiment of private fantasies and the fulfilment of private wishes. While she makes what she can of herself in a mercenary society and then struggles to keep herself going in a cruel world, her men in their various ways regard and treat her as a gratifying escape from it, though they also sometimes realise more or less clearly that she presents a constant threat to the constricting social order they have constructed for themselves. We should never forget that pre-First World War society was Wedekind's particular *bête noire* even in the Lulu plays, where it seems at first sight that erotic beauty is the destructive force that excites his wrath. Each man in Lulu's life seeks and finds in her what he wants or needs; but in none of them (except perhaps Dr Schön or, arguably, Jack the Ripper) does she find anything comparable. Each lets her down because he is flawed by a blind disregard for her true self, an indifference that stems from that blend of self-centredness and self-interest which Wedekind, like the great Austrian dramatist Grillparzer before him, saw as typically male, and which Lulu's partners never question because it is an integral part of the conventional thinking of their male-dominated society. To most of them Lulu's sex appeal is her sole *raison d'être*: for the elderly Dr Goll it provides titillation; for Schwarz, artistic inspiration; while glamour and pleasure are what Dr Schön sees and finds in her. But each tends to call her by pet names of his own invention, and to forget who she really is. Who is she really? Does even her old 'father' Schigolch really know? Perhaps she is just an emanation of the life-force (a concept much in vogue at the time) or a symbol of instinctual human joy whose flirtations with a series of egocentric individuals are simply part of the natural process, a dance of life as well as death. Only the Countess thinks differently, and she alone is selfless. But the drawback, of course, is that Lulu is not drawn to her. 'Damn!' says the Countess as she, too, dies. It is the drama's last word, and with it horror and comedy meet in rare conjunction.

The Lulu plays are a perplexing labyrinth, and much hot air has been vented on their meaning and significance. In their historical context, they make sense as a seminally productive variant of social realism in which axe-grinding earnestness and token verisimilitude are triumphantly replaced by unabashed theatricality. The imagery of their central stage property, Lulu's portrait, provides a cluster of thematically interrelated elements which give unity, but a unity subtle and elusive enough not to impair the feeling they convey of the sheer arbitrariness of 'real life'. Comic elements and farcical episodes abound in both plays, and, as in Restoration comedy, sex naturally provides the animating force and momentum underlying the playwright's burlesque treatment of the way the world treats a lovely woman.

But the Lulu plays have a tragic quality about them, too, which is probably easier to appreciate nowadays, when tragic ideals and aspirations have been tempered and deflated by the theatres of cruelty, silence and the absurd. Whatever the circumstances – and in the Lulu plays they are often ludicrous, risqué or even vulgar – the wanton destruction of something beautiful and intensely alive must always have a tragic impact. At the end of *Pandora's Box* the stage is as littered with corpses as in any Jacobean tragedy or *grand guignol* melodrama. Goll, Schwarz and Schön are dead already, and now Alwa is slain by Lulu's black London client, Chief Kungu Poti, while Lulu and the Countess end up the Ripper's victims. The sole survivor is old Schigolch, who is in many ways the most fascinating male figure in the plays, though he attracts scant critical attention. He first appears in Act II of *Earth Spirit*, when Schwarz mistakes him for an itinerant beggar (he claims to have taken part in a military campaign which may be identified as the 1866 'German War' between Austria and Prussia). From the start there is an other-worldly air about him, though he may appear to be just an old blackguard; destined to outlive them all, he tells Lulu at the very beginning that he is near unto death, and reminds her that 'we are dust'. In Act IV scene v, Rodrigo, the 'strong man', toasts him as 'Gevatter Tod' (Old Father Death) just after Lulu (in the preceding scene) has confessed her lifelong fear of death to Schön. Schigolch's allusions to mortality and decay take on wider dimensions in the closing scenes of *Pandora's Box*, where his talk reverts to the need for light amidst the gathering gloom – for, without Lulu, the light has gone out of the world.

What of Lulu herself? Like her admirers in the drama, critics see her in many different lights. To some she is predatory and destructive, to others vulnerable and naïve. She has been described as fascinating and as repulsive, the amoral embodiment of sexual instinct, a female Don Juan, an innocent corruptress of decent social standards, a vamp, a spoilt child, a sort of doll – or a courageous woman who lives life on her own terms, but falls victim to a rapacious, violent, male-dominated society. She may be some or, indeed, all of these things; the emphasis has always varied from actress to actress, from production to production. But she may also be more besides, as the titles of the two plays suggest. She may be an incarnation of the life-force and the embodiment of all that men's senses crave; the eternal object of the sexual urge; the irresistible personification of earthly joys as well as an ordinary woman. Is she Eve, the mother of all our sins and Adam's undoing? Or is she Pandora, according to classical mythology the first woman ever created, whose heart the gods filled with perfidy and lies, and who brought with her into the world a mysterious box which held countless afflictions for the human race? Wedekind's Prologue to *Earth Spirit*, which many critics emphasise at the expense of the plays, goes one step further, and equates Lulu with the serpent in the Garden of Eden, 'created for every abuse, to allure and to poison and seduce'.

Lulu must certainly be seductive. The role is one where personality and appearance are at a premium, for if a Lulu fails to convince her audience that she is irresistible, the drama collapses. Most of the time she is the only woman on stage, and most of the other characters define themselves almost entirely through their responses to her: neither she nor they have much to fall back on by way of other interest or motivation. But her beauty and her sex-appeal lie in presentation rather than in the words of the text, which are colourless and flat, little more than an all-purpose script which requires much extraneous and simultaneous detail to fill it out before the role can be fully realised. In this respect Wedekind is in marked contrast to Hauptmann or Schnitzler, who both excel in capturing and conveying mood and motivation through the speech of their characters, especially when their plays are set in the socio-linguistic locations they knew best. Wedekind did not possess their ear for the psychological dimensions of spoken language. Perhaps because he grew up in dialect-speaking Switzerland, he was not as attuned as they were to the idiomatic subtleties of modern German as spoken by people in Austria and Germany. This may have been something of a disadvantage, yet it also gave him one distinct advantage: his work loses much less in translation than theirs, which in turn may well account for the relatively greater success he has enjoyed abroad.

Thematically the Lulu plays do have their parallels in the work of Hauptmann and Schnitzler. The comparison with *The Round Dance* is telling. The male characters in the Lulu plays have counterparts of sorts in the Schnitzler play, since it was the aim of both dramatists to include all sorts and conditions of men; the obvious difference is that in Schnitzler's play the 'eternal feminine' is forever re-embodied in well-differentiated individual women, whereas in Wedekind's it is concentrated in the protagonist, who therefore has to be all things to all men. Closer to Wedekind's conception is Hauptmann's fascinating play *And Pippa Dances!* (*Und Pippa tanzt!*, 1906), which was written for and inspired by Ida Orloff, a talented young actress who had already appeared in a minor role in the 1905 Vienna production of *Pandora's Box*. Hauptmann became enthralled by her when he saw her 'become' his own imaginary character Hannele. Pippa, the role he wrote for her, represents the ideal of elusive femininity to an assortment of men, but, in order to pursue this theme without actually implying that all women are really the same, Hauptmann soon diverges from both Wedekind and Schnitzler by leaving the plane of common reality behind and entering a fantasy world in which poetic licence is permissible and symbolism can weave its spells unhindered.

The all-purpose, almost 'acquired' feel of Wedekind's language, together with the ease with which his text can be adapted and pruned, have undoubtedly stood the two Lulu plays in good stead in the theatre. Though he gave them a framework of topical allusions, updating is no great problem and demonstrates the drama's continuing relevance. In Wedekind's own lifetime, Lulu was an Edwardian or *fin-de-siècle* demi-mondaine; in the 1902 Berlin production Gertrud Eysoldt presented her as a soulless, sophisticated modern version of Salome; in Vienna in 1905 Tilly Newes, later to become Wedekind's wife, brought out her latent tenderness and femininity; while, a little later, Maria Orska's Lulu was the white-faced pierrot doll. Then, in 1928, G. W. Pabst's silent film *Die Büchse der Pandora* allowed Louise Brooks (1906–85) to project an image of Lulu 1920s style – indeed this film has led many people to assume that the plays were in fact a product of that era. Changing attitudes to women, as well as to public and private morality, have naturally resulted in shifts of emphasis, and this is reflected in more recent stage-interpretations. The circus element, with Wedekind as ringmaster and Lulu as tamed beast, present in the Prologue but only very intermittently in the main text, has inspired some productions, while others have brought out the elements of burlesque and farce which do indeed gain the upper hand at various points even in the original text.

Are the Lulu plays a closely structured period piece? Or is Wedekind's text an open invitation to experimentation and reinterpretation? At one point Wedekind claimed, rather tongue-in-cheek, that the Lesbian Countess was the true tragic heroine of the plays; if enough of the text is cut, no doubt the second play can be presented successfully even in this way. Given pace, zest, colour, movement, good ensemble, and a wild and lovely actress in the title role, there is no doubt that Wedekind's masterpiece still works and can prove itself to be a winner.

'The Marquis von Keith'

Der Marquis von Keith received its first performance in 1901 at the Residenz-Theater in Berlin, a house which specialised in lighter French contemporary social comedy but occasionally ventured beyond Sardou to Ibsen and Strindberg. Though Wedekind had by now acquired a reputation for the *outré*, his new play had superficial similarities with the type of play the theatre liked, and his obvious dramatic gifts made the risk seem worth taking.

The subject of the play is the age-old one of a vainglorious trickster's short-lived triumph at the expense of his gullible victims, and his eventual unmasking. Its plot – a simple one of rise and fall – has obvious affinities to, say, Molière's *Tartuffe*, though it dispenses with intrigue in the grand comic manner. Symmetry is evident everywhere. The characters complement each other or provide contrast to one another, and at the centre is the self-styled Marquis von Keith, a complete nonentity who has outrageously assumed a name which was very much one to be reckoned with in the Germany of Kaiser

Wilhelm: it belonged to a distinguished Prussian military and aristocratic family which could trace its origins back to Scottish Jacobite soldiers of fortune. The 'Marquis' certainly shares with his alleged ancestors an eye for the main chance, an ability to live off his wits, and an unquenchable confidence in his own good luck even if fighting in a lost cause – that of his own financial and social success.

The extrovert would-be marquis is given a foil in the person of Ernst Scholz, an introverted young man devoid of self-confidence who, despite his ordinary name, is in fact a genuine aristocrat whose real name is Count Trautmann; the two young men grew up together on the family estate, and soon discovered that they complemented each other in character as well as in their backgrounds and prospects. The women in the play are grouped symmetrically around the protagonist, and they, too, are effectively contrasted. Molly, his eighteen-year-old girlfriend, has given up her respectable middle-class background and home in the provinces to run off with him, but in the end is dropped and makes away with herself, while his mistress, a voluptuous beauty of thirty who was once a shop assistant called Anna Huber, but is now an aspiring Wagnerian soprano named Countess Werdenfels, just as ruthlessly drops him as soon as he is finally exposed for what he really is – a man hardly able, let alone likely, to sponsor her 'artistic' aspirations any further.

When the play begins, the 'Marquis' is confident that his grandiose plan to mastermind the construction of a vast new entertainment complex in Munich is about to be realised – it turns out, of course, to be as insubstantial as its proposed name, the Fairy Palace, implies. By the end of the play his pretensions have been revealed for the sham they are, though 10,000 marks in banknotes from the people he has duped and defrauded helps to expedite his sudden departure from Munich before the full truth dawns on its citizens. To be given adequate financial means to live on into the twentieth century (the action takes place during the summer of 1899) recommends itself to the erstwhile 'Marquis' as a rather better option than the obvious and honourable alternative, suicide; for a moment he hesitates between the cash and his revolver, then with a smile he puts the revolver down on the table. 'Life is full of ups and downs,' he observes as the curtain falls. We do not see him actually pick up the money, a touch which shows Wedekind the (tragi-) comedy playwright at his best.

Keith's shady dealings and flamboyant life-style serve to caricature and expose the values of a society founded almost exclusively on wealth, where to be better off rather than worse off is really all that matters. He manipulates all those with whom he comes into contact, and does so with consummate ease and social know-how because, as he says, 'you can really only do good business within the framework of society as it is'. He is no revolutionary playing the capitalist game for all it is worth while working away to undermine the *status quo*, and society recognises this by letting him off lightly; at the end of the play he is discountenanced but unscathed, and no doubt ready to seek fresh pastures for his double-dealing. 'Any ass can have bad luck: the art is to know how to make the most of it and turn it to one's advantage.' Keith has the art he prizes, and delights in performing his balancing-act on the tightrope of improvisation, with exposure threatening at every step. 'Truth', he tells Scholz, 'is our most precious possession, and one cannot be too sparing with it. Tell people what they want to hear, and you'll be able to get what you want out of them.' Up to a point he succeeds by taking his own advice.

The other main characters in the play do not possess the protagonist's dubious virtues. Molly, his girlfriend, is hopelessly dominated by him although she has seen through him: love, as Wedekind is always fond of telling us, obscures clarity of vision. Countess Werdenfels is less infatuated with the man and more taken with his money; when she realises he has none, she naturally sees him quite clearly for what he is and drops him, an ironic but convincing comment on the play's central theme. Ernst Scholz, the aristocrat who aspires to be an average man, does all he can to model himself on Keith and be his understudy, but in the end his efforts fail: it is so very much easier for a bad man to appear good than for a good man to be bad, he discovers – thus making nonsense of the commonly held view that it is supremely easy to be wicked or immoral, but a constant struggle to be virtuous, a view which could only be held by a respectable society whose members are all, in Wedekind's view, rogues. With considerable irony, again, though of a more drastic sort, Ernst Scholz ends up in a private mental clinic whereas his model and hero accepts the world for what it is and therefore survives. Yet Keith, too, has his defects. Wedekind, himself an actor with an eye for the telling touch, gives him a limp, which may remind some members of the audience of the Devil: after all, the Devil is said to have invented the theatre in order to reveal what goes on behind the scenes of bourgeois life, or so we read in Lesage's satirical novel *Le Diable boiteux* (1707). In keeping with contemporary realism, this physical handicap is also used to motivate Keith's deep-seated psychological urge to get the better of other people. These double associations, with their blend of realism and allegorical symbol, are characteristic of Wedekind's drama.

Typical, too, is the tendency of Wedekind's dialogue to move towards abstraction, especially in the scenes involving Keith and his friend Scholz. One of the best of these occurs in Act IV, when earnest young Scholz is agonising over the difficulty of becoming what he calls 'a useful member of society', and prompts his less scrupulous companion to give an account of his own, less altruistic view of life. British audiences will at once be reminded of Shaw, and, like Shaw, Wedekind can be very funny: for example, when time is running out for him,

Keith implores Scholz to give him money, unobtrusively raising the sum by 10,000 each time he renews his entreaties. Wedekind also exploits the stock techniques of farce to offset what might otherwise have been preponderantly verbal comedy: doors open and close to conceal or admit characters some of whom happen to overhear what others wish to hide. But these amusing techniques are not just used to entertain the audience; they are also used to a serious end and to keep the producer on his toes, since they effectively translate the central themes of deception, pretence, concealment and exposure into stage action and movement.

Particularly effective and original is the use of a firework display in Act III to provide ironic counterpoint both visually and audibly to the conversations going on between Anna Werdenfels and Keith and between Molly and Scholz during the lavish party being thrown by the 'Marquis' to launch his grandiose cultural project, the 'Fairy Palace': for example, '*KEITH kisses ANNA rapturously, while in the garden a firework flares up, illuminating the couple for a moment in a dark-red glow*', or 'Let me tell you, I'm a believer (*in the garden a rocket whizzes up into the sky*), and I devoutly believe that our labours and sacrifices are rewarded – in this world.' Wedekind's purpose here is to spotlight the hollowness of his characters' words and actions, and in doing so to reveal the 'true' values of the affluent society of his day; the fireworks are an amusing counterpart to the famous explosions which rock the last act of Shaw's *Heartbreak House* (1917) as the German Zeppelins fly overhead. Audiences were not amused by Wedekind's antics, however. It is hardly surprising that, at least until after the First World War, his ridicule of them and their comfortably, complacently well-to-do world met with their hostility. Not until the war did his play enjoy anything like popularity, but by then, of course, the way of life Wedekind had caricatured was beginning to crumble.

The Marquis von Keith is a dramatic *tour de force* and the role of its protagonist an actor's challenge (brilliantly taken up, for example, by Leonard Rossiter), but it does not stand entirely alone in modern German drama. Its tone and approach provided a model for the sequence of plays written between 1911 and 1916 in which Wedekind's own well-to-do son-in-law Carl Sternheim (1878–1942; he married Wedekind's daughter Pamela) set about sending up middle-class stuffiness, smugness and stupidity, and which he grouped together under the general title *Scenes from the Heroic Life of the Middle Classes* (*Aus dem bürgerlichen Heldenleben*). *The Marquis von Keith* was also a brilliant variation on a theme which has often enjoyed particular popularity in the German-speaking countries – the portrayal of confidence tricksters and their ultimate exposure. Carl Zuckmayer (1896–1977), a playwright more in the Gerhart Hauptmann mould, took this type of play a stage further by creating Germany's classic military variation on the theme, *The Captain of Köpenick* (*Der Hauptmann von Köpenick*). Produced in 1931, but based on a real-life episode which took place in 1906, this play about a comic con-man turned out to be one of the major box-office successes in Germany during the years immediately before the political promises of Hitler took in the majority of the German population.

'The Tenor'

Wedekind's one-act play *The Tenor* (*Der Kammersänger*) was published in 1899 and performed the same year at a special matinée in Berlin together with a one-acter by his less famous contemporary, Wilhelm von Scholz. In later revivals it was often given in conjunction with other, better-known plays such as Schnitzler's *Liebelei*, Sudermann's *Fritzchen* (about a boy faced with the imminent prospect of death in a duel), or Oscar Wilde's

101

Salomé or *A Florentine Tragedy*; between the wars, Strindberg was felt to be more appropriate, and nowadays Anouilh's *L'Orchestre* is the usual choice in German theatres. The first public production of *The Tenor* took place in Leipzig in 1900, and the play soon established itself as an effective and cost-effective stage-work for small ensemble; it needs little in the way of properties or sets, and, unusually for Wedekind, it has never aroused much outrage or hostility on moral grounds. This does not mean to say that it is dull. On the contrary, its success was confirmed by its revival at Max Reinhardt's Neues Theater in 1903, and it has always remained a favourite with the public, although Wedekind did not greatly care for it himself. Of all his plays it is still the one most frequently revived in the German-speaking world; but outside that cultural orbit its appeal has always been more limited, because its subject exploits a lofty conception of art and the artist which is peculiarly German. Indeed, in the gentlest way is debunks what has been one of Germany's fondest notions ever since the Romantic age – the sacrosanctity of art – and at the same time satirises the cultural snobbery inherent in the tenor's official title, which is the German title of the play itself: *Der Kammersänger*.

The scene is a room in a hotel. The central figure, a *Heldentenor* named Gerardo, has just sung the part of Tannhäuser in Wagner's opera, and is attempting to spend a quiet three-quarters of an hour looking over the score of *Tristan and Isolde* before leaving for Brussels where he is shortly due to sing the role of Tristan. Wedekind's sense of humour is much to the fore as, time and time again, the hapless Gerardo is disturbed in this sublime yet also pre-eminently urgent task by a succession of clearly contrasted but essentially complementary visitors. The first is a sixteen-year-old English girl who rejoices in the name of Miss Isabel Coeurne. Her infatuation with him – or rather, with Wagner's romantic Knight of the Swan in *Lohengrin* – obliges the tenor, who is quite a pleasant fellow at heart, to try his best to convince her that he is nothing but the mouthpiece of the Master. 'Study his texts and learn to feel the meaning of his leitmotifs,' he advises; 'try to get interested in opera instead of the men on the stage.' This gently-made point about the fundamental discrepancy between the play and the player earns from Miss Coeurne a faint 'I thank you.'

The next visitor causes rather more disturbance. This time the tenor is buttonholed by an elderly and very Teutonic musicologist who has poured out his innermost soul into an opera which he hopes Gerardo will sing. Almost drowned by Professor Dühring's outpouring of elevated self-pity, Gerardo asks him – most unwisely – to play the work through: there happens, of course, to be a piano in his room.

The scene which ensues is one of the funniest Wedekind ever wrote. The desperate efforts of the old fellow to locate the best bits in his voluminous score merely serve to give a grotesquely disjointed impression of a profoundly unified work of the kind which no one in an audience would ever wish to have to listen to from beginning to end. With croaking voice he sings what then turns out to be a chorus, and the disparity between its high-flown words and his well-meant but inept presentation is ludicrous. 'Is that music?' he interrupts himself, gazing wide-eyed at Gerardo. 'Possibly,' the tenor replies. His attempts to extricate himself from the situation are of no avail. 'In other words you mean that my music is old-fashioned,' says the Professor. 'No, quite the opposite; I should rather say it's very modern,' the embarrassed tenor replies. The topicality of such exchanges will be evident to anyone aware of what was taking place on the musical scene in Germany at the turn of the century – Schoenberg's *Verklärte Nacht* (*Transfigured Night*) and Richard Strauss's *Feuersnot* (*Fire-Famine*) date from the same year. The continuing relevance of the scene to developments in modern music has raised laughs ever since.

Soon, however, the play moves towards a more abstract presentation of ideas associated with the theme of art; what emerges most forcefully are the pressures under which professional performers such as Gerardo have to exist: public and publishers both have requirements which the poor performing artist must fulfil, and his timetable makes his artistic life even more hectic. A generous offer of 500 marks helps to get the self-styled composer on his way, but he then declines the money. Perhaps he was a genius after all?

Gerardo's third visitor (a piano teacher hiding behind a screen hardly counts!) is the lovely Helena Marowa, who bursts in with a passionate ultimatum: 'Either take me with you, or I die!' But the drawback is that Gerardo's contract forbids him to marry or to travel with a lady. She simply cannot comprehend this. How could he ever have agreed to such a stipulation? 'I am an artist first and foremost, and only then am I a man,' Gerardo replies, not without a trace of self-satisfaction. Trying every argument he can think of, and with time running out before his train, he manages to calm her down and win her round; she promises to behave herself and to return to her womanly responsibilities as a wife and mother – in a word, to give him up. Then – *coup de théâtre*! – she draws a revolver from her muff and shoots herself. Gerardo thinks all is lost. But the hotel manager is suavely reassuring: 'Please do not worry, sir; things like this happen here quite often. . . .' The tenor rushes off to his waiting cab: Wagner's *Tristan* with its famous 'Liebestod' awaits him. This being a comedy, there is no reason to assume that the lovely young lady lying on the bedroom carpet is really dead, though, of course, productions keen to stress the underlying seriousness of Wedekind's purpose take a more drastic and macabre view.

'Hidalla'

Some people consider *Hidalla*, subtitled 'Karl Hetman; or, The Stunted Giant', to be Wedekind's best play. Its first performance took place in Munich in 1905, with Wedekind himself in the title role, but it was Victor Barnowsky's production at the Kleines Theatre, Berlin, later that year, with Wedekind again in the lead role, that really created a stir. It ran for fifty performances, and inaugurated a stage success which continued well into the 1920s. It is seldom if ever performed today.

The play concerns a group of people whose attempt to set up a modern sociological research institute becomes involved with the self-imposed mission of an eccentric individual, Karl Hetman, to promote an international association for breeding racially perfect human beings. Wedekind wrote the part of Hetman for himself, and by all accounts it was one of his best roles as an actor. 'This amateur was the only real human being on stage: the rest were little more than puppets,' wrote one reviewer. 'As long as he was there in front of us, we forgot everything else,' wrote another.

Even now we can still sense something of the sardonic humour tinged with pathos inherent in the part. Hetman is a man whose mind is filled with visions of a better future, when people will come to value beauty above their lives and possessions, wars will cease, and peace and harmony prevail; but his outward appearance immediately strikes a discordant note. '*Hetman*', reads the stage-direction when he first appears, '*is a person of deformed and unprepossessing appearance, smooth-shaven, toothless, with thin hair and large eyes ablaze with passion.*' Yet he possesses charisma, and for a while comes to dominate the others. Until, that is, he overreaches himself. His contribution to the research institute's journal, a learned article on 'love-life in bourgeois society compared with that of our domestic pets', leads to its confiscation for indecency and earns him six months in jail. By Act III his grandiose schemes have all disintegrated, and he realises why. His calculations were false, for the priorities of the majority of human beings will always remain unalterably the same: wealth means more to them than the quality of life; for women, beauty is merely a means to an end; and young people really hanker after security, not after challenges and the thrill of taking glorious risks. After a public meeting at which one of his erstwhile supporters denounces him as a madman, he is committed to a mental hospital, but after six months he is released, because medically speaking he is perfectly sane.

By the last act of the play it seems that his star is rising again and that his ability to win popularity is undiminished. But a tragic anagnorisis of the most blackly humorous kind is in store for him. A gentleman calls to see him and offers the most generous terms for his services. Hetman is gratified, but then discovers that the gentleman is a circus director who hopes that by engaging Hetman as a clown or fall guy he will have an effective counter-attraction to the star turn of a rival circus: a chimpanzee that can sing the scale of C major. The mockery here is at once comic and shattering. Seared to the core by the implicit equation between himself, an ugly little human being with noble aspirations, and an ape with the ability to mimic a man, Hetman realises that he has made a complete fool of himself. Fanny, the good-looking and intelligent woman who really loves him, and Herr Launert, the self-styled social scientist who has ruthlessly exploited him, enter simultaneously and find him hanging behind a curtain in his washing cubicle. The dead man has left behind him the manuscript of a book entitled 'Hidalla; or, The Morality of Beauty'. Launert seizes it, gleefully looking forward to editing and publishing it, and to all the profits he will reap: after all, its author's suicide makes excellent publicity. Fanny lies cowering at his feet as the curtain falls.

The central action of *Hidalla* has obvious connections with much of Wedekind's finest and most characteristic work; it may even be said to fuse elements from plays as disparate as *Earth Spirit*, *Pandora's Box* and *The Marquis von Keith* (for example, the beauty–ugliness syndrome; the con-man; the circus) into an effectively rounded stage play which transcends these other works in its tragi-comic implications. The central character is certainly an extraordinary achievement. Uniquely memorable, Hetman is at one and the same time intensely individual and also typically representative of the human species with all its peculiar paradoxes, a species which paradoxically he would like to purify and metamorphose into something higher, though he himself retains the petty foibles and shortcomings of an average, ordinary person. Indeed, the dimensions of his role and character have expanded enormously since the play opened in 1905. One has only to think of the uncomfortable parallels betweeen this ugly little man's incongruous obsession with thoroughbred racial purity, and the ideology promoted by Adolf Hitler, to realise that this remarkable German play contains disturbingly prophetic implications which no one, not even its author, could have appreciated thirty years before the Nuremberg race laws were promulgated in 1935. Needless to say, *Hidalla* was not revived under the Third Reich.

Around his tragi-comic protagonist's rise and fall, Wedekind groups a set of well-differentiated characters who all relate to him in one way or another, and who bring out the complex interplay of abstract issues and vested interests which always fascinated the dramatist, but which he did not always succeed in embodying in such convincingly drawn men and women. Thus the intrinsic beauty of Fanny, both physically and morally, is offset by Berta Launert, clever but plain, while Launert himself, slick and successful, is contrasted with his gormless but well-meaning business partner, Herr Gellinghausen. A plump, blue-blooded German princess and an angular American millionairess both dote on the handsome yet mindless male model whom Hetman utilises to illustrate his racial ideal – a situation which provokes some entertaining by-play. It is a great pity that this once popular Wedekind play has fallen out of the repertoire in Germany and Austria, and that it has never been given a chance on the English-speaking stage. Its verve, grotesque humour and ludicrous yet grippingly moving *dénouement* could still exert appeal, its central themes are still relevant, and the stunted giant at its centre, into whom Wedekind put so much of himself and which he originally created, might prove a rewarding role for a British or American comic actor.

'King Nicolo' and 'Music'

Two of Wedekind's other plays deserve mention. *Such is Life* (*So ist das Leben*), later known as *King Nicolo* (*König Nicolo*), was first performed in 1902 in Munich and 1903 in Berlin. It may be regarded as something of a concession to prevailing taste because, uncharacteristically, it is a pseudo-historical costume drama set in Renaissance Italy: this was an extremely fashionable setting for operas and plays at the turn of the century – other examples are Maeterlinck's *Monna Vanna* (1902) and Schnitzler's *The Veil of Beatrice* (*Der Schleier der Beatrice*, 1900). In Wedekind's contribution to this vogue, a deposed king travels around his erstwhile realm disguised as a strolling player. He tries to express his personal situation and suffering in the form of tragedy, but the spectators find it funny; instead, he has recourse to comedy, and this earns him an ironic reward: he is made the fool or court jester of the very man – a former master-butcher – who has usurped the throne. The personal note is unmistakably audible in this play, even though at first sight it seems far removed from the up-to-date topics and racy style of Wedekind's more characteristic satirical plays. In fact the pathos of his creative life – genuine enough even if enhanced by a good deal of self-dramatisation – comes over with especially bitter force in the 'on with the motley' theme which permeates the play and offsets the influence of extravagant neo-Romantic make-believe.

King Nicolo has been revived sporadically in Germany with varying success: interestingly and perhaps significantly, it was the only Wedekind play to be staged there during the Nazi period (Kassel, 1939), when the dramatist's work was considered decadent. Maybe the remoteness of its Renaissance setting made it acceptable and obscured the possibility that spectators might identify the demoted actor-monarch with the stifled voice of the regime's opponents and the usurping master-butcher with the Führer himself.

Wedekind's other main play, *Music* (*Musik*), first performed in 1908 in Nuremberg, illustrates a similar tragi-comic dichotomy but is more obviously a development of the type of play he had already made his own. A young woman encumbered with the clumsy name of Klara Hühnerwadel is being cynically coached by a singing-teacher to believe that she is likely to become a great Wagnerian soprano; but his tuition has other, less uplifting consequences. Klara is found guilty of seeking an abortion, but is pardoned in response to the pleas of the singing-teacher's wife, who takes pity on the girl; he, for his part, would gladly be rid of her despite the fact that she has given him all her money. Once again she announces that she is pregnant. This time she boldly decides to have the child – but it dies within days. A further bitter irony shatters her: her own mother, ignorant of the true circumstances, thanks the singing-teacher for all the help and support he has given her daughter and then rounds on the hapless writer who had genuinely tried to assist her. Wedekind subtitled the play a 'portrayal of contemporary manners', and he paints them with indignant humour. When clumsy, sensitive Klara accepts the double standards of contemporary society, she is forgiven; but when she decides to assert herself and stand up for her own moral values, the opposite happens, and society's representatives condemn her.

In subject and plot *Music* has affinities with Hauptmann's realistic drama *Rose Bernd* (1902), and many earlier productions stressed this aspect; but it cannot be pursued too far. As Max Reinhardt once commented, Wedekind cannot be played like Gerhart Hauptmann: he needs a special style of his own. *Music* was not written out of compassion, and it radiates no emotional warmth; as Wedekind knew, his work lacked the love, the human sympathy, which informs the work of his rival. His own play presents a squalid everyday 'tragedy' for what it is and invites us to watch it and consider its implications with laughter rather than tears, and, above all, with detachment. Klara's doctor has what may be taken as the last word when he dispassionately observes, 'Unfortunately I have often noticed, when misfortune strikes, that when it is at its most unfortunate, it often starts to make one laugh.'

3
Arthur Schnitzler

Schnitzler on Theatre

I feel that it is my job to create human beings; I have nothing to prove except how very varied the world is. In the last resort, the secret of all dramatic energy lies in knowing how to work out a plot so that each and every character involved in it, or who just impinges on it, is compelled to reveal his or her most intimate being. The ordering of events depends to some extent on the writer's artistic intentions and probably also on his theatrical preferences; but the main characters and certainly the hero (let us retain the old term!) cannot be put together bit by bit just on impulse or when they happen to be needed. They must be there right from the start, exactly as they materialized in the author's mind, and their development must continue along exactly the same lines. (Letter to Richard Charmatz, 1913)

Hauptmann on Schnitzler

Arthur Schnitzler's mellow and delicate art has something about it which is rather rare in Germany: charm. Its charm isn't

111

French, it is German. His plays and his characters never ever force themselves on you in any way; as a result he may sometimes seem rather pallid. We are constantly going to have to revise our opinion of him so as not to lose sight of the distinctive colouring and great beauties of his work, and save it as part of our German heritage. Appreciation of Schnitzler is equivalent to being cultured, and to be drawn to him is to be in search of culture. He should be played far more frequently than he is. (1922)

Wedekind on Schnitzler
Arthur Schnitzler is a German classic. The characteristic hallmark of his works is the masterly way in which their dénouements are reached. Not one line in them seems dated. (1912)

Introduction

Schnitzler embodies Vienna in much the same way as James Joyce embodies Dublin. His plays and stories captured his city so vividly and compellingly that we owe our idea of Vienna, or at least of it as it was, in very large measure to his works and to the films and television productions based on them. There were other writers in Ireland besides Joyce, and Schnitzler, likewise, was by no means the only writer active in the Vienna of his day. The high ground of drama and lyric poetry was occupied by Hugo von Hofmannsthal, whose text for the opera *Der Rosenkavalier* (1911) by Richard Strauss also helped to convey to a wide international public a quality very characteristic of the city – its *joie de vivre* often tinged with nostalgia for a grander past and apprehension about the future. A mood of bitter-sweetness became characteristic of Viennese literature and music, even lighter works such as the operetta *Die Fledermaus*

(1874) by Johann Strauss. Many other poets, writers and intellectuals moved in the same sophisticated *fin-de-siècle* circles as Hofmannsthal, but it was Schnitzler who excelled all his competitors when it came to finding the right words to convey what it felt like to be part of the city which, still 1918, was the administrative centre of much of the Austro-Hungarian Empire. The waltzes and operettas of Strauss, Millöcker and Lehár had carried its romanticised image all over the world, but it was also a metropolis of some 1,650,000 inhabitants where many of the most serious problems of modern life were manifesting themselves and were being discussed by thoughtful people.

Arthur Schnitzler was born in 1862, the same year as Gerhart Hauptmann. His father was a successful doctor who later pioneered an outpatients' clinic in Vienna and became a distinguished specialist in diseases of the larynx, an area in which his son also specialised, somewhat reluctantly, during his years of medical study and practice before he emerged as a writer; even his Viennese contemporary Freud (to whom he bore an uncanny resemblance) was ready to recognise his powers of clinical observation and to admire his insight into the subconscious motivations of his characters. Schnitzler's background was entirely medical, but it is also significant to note that his father had come to Vienna as a medical student from a humble social background in south-west Hungary; the name Schnitzler actually means 'woodcarver', and for generations the family had been joiners – trade names of this kind were frequently adopted by Jews or imposed on them by the authorities. By the time his son was being educated at a good Vienna grammar school, the Schnitzlers had become fully assimilated, though, like many other educated, medically orientated and free-thinking Jews, they had resisted conversion to Roman Catholicism, the dominant religion of Austria and her empire. It would be mistaken, however, to give undue emphasis to Schnitzler's Jewishness; it seldom impinges directly on his plays; his diaries reveal that, although he was always acutely conscious of it, it played no very great part in his artistic life except during the wave of anti-semitism which swept Vienna in the 1890s. His impressive 'medical' drama *Professor Bernhardi* (1912) is based on an episode which occurred then, and is his only major play to turn on this issue. If Schnitzler had lived longer, things might have been very different, but he died in 1931, just before the rising tide of National Socialism had begun to affect literature in Germany or the Austrian Republic, of which Vienna had become the capital in 1918. Schnitzler's creative life spans the period from 1890 to 1930, with the earlier years from 1890 to 1914 looming larger because it was the spirit of this era, the Austrian equivalent of Britain's Edwardian Age and of *la belle époque* in France, that his genius most uniquely captures and immortalises.

Schnitzler arrived as a playwright in 1895 when, on 9 October, his three-act play *Liebelei* opened at the Burgtheater, the leading theatre in the Austrian capital and indeed in the entire German-speaking world. It aroused such interest that it was taken up by the Deutsches Theater in Berlin early in 1896. Over forty plays followed – the exact number varies because Schnitzler left some dramatic sketches incomplete, while other dramatic works, such as *Anatol*, consist of a number of almost independent components. Of the grand total of forty, a smaller number form the body of work on which Schnitzler's reputation as a dramatist depends; his standing as a novelist and short-story writer is another matter. In Austria and, to a lesser extent, in the German-speaking world generally, the accepted canon of Schnitzler plays includes several whose appeal depends on the fact that they deal with their subjects in ways which have meaning and relevance at home, though not abroad; like some good wines, they do not travel well. *The Lonely Way* and *The Vast Domain* are obvious cases, and *Professor Bernhardi* is another, although for different reasons. Schnitzler's output also includes a group of plays which are seldom if ever performed today, but command respect as literature: *Paracelsus* and *The Veil of Beatrice* (*Der Schleier der Beatrice*) are poetic dramas in the grand manner, and *Young Medardus* (*Der junge Medardus*) treats subject matter associated with the Napoleonic era as seen through Austrian eyes. Both the content of these plays and their particular type of theatricality stand in the way of international acceptance. This, however, is certainly not the case with the ironic, bitter-sweet Viennese plays with which Schnitzler's name is particularly associated: *Anatol*, *Liebelei* and *The Round Dance*. It is with these that an account of Austria's first major modern dramatist must begin.

'Anatol'

Anatol is a cycle of one-act playlets written between 1888 and 1891, and containing virtually all the themes and features that are now associated with Schnitzler's evocation of *fin-de-siècle* Vienna. They are more thoughtful than at first sight appears: the frivolous tone belies an underlying seriousness.

Each playlet presents one of Anatol's brief and usually final encounters with a succession of well-differentiated but equally attractive women – Cora, Gabriele, Bianca (alias Bibi), Emilie, Annie, Else, Ilona and Annette – each of whom highlights facets of feminine psychology in relation to Anatol's own consistent personality, of which, however, he (unlike the author) is only intermittently aware. One senses that Schnitzler put a good deal of himself into this prototype of so many of his Viennese male characters, and that in this early set of plays he was working on the assumption that the self-scrutiny involved in painting a self-portrait was the most direct method of paring away the cherished assumptions of both his own ego and of dramatic fiction in general, and getting down to the reality underneath. The task was undertaken at the risk of revealing Anatol's defects: his childishly incorrigible self-esteem, for instance, and his shallow responses to emotional claims as well as his endemic tendency to demand total faithfulness from the women in his life yet expect the opposite. In Anatol's case self-scrutiny is complemented and assisted by the presence of his detached friend Max, an adaptation of the stock *raisonneur* figure of nineteenth-century social drama, who here also becomes an effective manifestation of the more rational and realistic level of the playwright's own psyche.

In the course of the cycle the composite male personality represented by the attitudes of Max and Anatol is brought into contact or collision with a series of female characters, whose differences of attitude and approach are relatively slight in comparison to the basic femininity they all have in common. Just as Anatol and Max stand for the male way of seeing, feeling and behaving, especially in relation to women, so the different women present us with related facets of the female psyche in relation to men. To each and all of them in their differing ways Anatol represents a chance of emotional freedom and emancipation: he is the eternally attractive lover, a playboy and *bon vivant* in sharp contrast to their predictable, dull husbands, their steady boyfriends, and that host of average males who lack Anatol's charm, his intensity alternating with indifference, and his apparent wish to live a life devoted to the pleasures of the moment rather than find permanence and security in any one relationship. Indeed it is precisely this that attracts Anatol's women friends and enables them to forget conventional attitudes and commitments when they are in his company.

Such frank portrayal of a man represented something of a breakthrough in European drama. Anatol may not be a hero, but he is not a villain either; he may be a philanderer, yet he is not presented as a cad, caddish though his conduct might appear to the conventional husbands off stage, to whom it is the fate of his more respectable mistresses to be married. While apparently directing the attention of its audience to a delightful set of variations on the perennial theme of what Goethe called 'das ewig Weibliche' (the eternal feminine), Schnitzler's first dramatic venture should more properly be seen as an original fusion of revue and monodrama, with, as its centre of interest, the character of Anatol and the way he copes with his sequence of romantic problems. A production conceived in such terms, with a leading actor fully up to the demands of the title role, would be in line with Schnitzler's intentions. The role of Max, too, makes special demands on the actor. He has a vital part to play in his dialogues with Anatol, which are usually situated at the beginning of each playlet, but when Anatol's current lady-friend enters, he either leaves the stage or remains present but silent – no doubt a production problem in amateur performance, though of course a challenge for actors with a command of gesture and facial expression. From the theatrical point of view *Anatol* is in fact something of a test-piece and very much a product of the period in which Schnitzler was writing: each brief episode must generate its own intimate atmosphere – for example the autumnal evening in *Mementoes* (*Denksteine*) or the late-nineteenth-century fashionable street scene in *Christmas Shopping* (*Weihnachtseinkäufe*) – and each must be perfectly in tune with the personality of the lady concerned and the emotional problem she presents for Anatol. There are other production hurdles, too. Most obviously, perhaps, these arise in the most deftly turned of all the episodes, *A Farewell Supper* (*Abschiedssouper*), the fifth in the cycle. In this playlet, Anatol's 'last supper' with his already superseded girlfriend Annie takes place at ten in the evening in a *cabinet particulier* at Sacher's, that most elegant of Viennese restaurants, to the accompaniment, throughout, of a waiter's entrances and exits; all the exchanges take place while Anatol,

Annie and Max are consuming a mouthwatering collation which starts with Ostend oysters and goes on to *filet aux truffes*, washed down with plenty of claret and champagne – a counterpart in glamorous miniature of the memorable dinner in Hauptmann's *Before Sunrise*, written in 1889. Schnitzler sets his actors the considerable task of co-ordinating their repartee, their shifting moods and the serving and consumption of food and drink in such a way as to convey the impression that all this is the most natural thing in the world.

Of the seven playlets that form the *Anatol* cycle, *A Farewell Supper* is the most immediately appealing because of its blend of farce and tragi-comedy, realism and stylised sophistication. The cycle opens with a playlet touching on a topic which was arousing great interest at the time, and which Schnitzler was closely concerned with in his capacity as a man of science. *A Question to Destiny* (*Die Frage an das Schicksal*) turns on hypnosis, and its composition coincided with his major medical publication, 'Über funktionelle Aphonie und ihre Behandlung durch Hypnose und Suggestion', a study of loss of speech and its treatment by means of hypnosis, which appeared in 1889 in the *Internationale klinische Rundschau*, a medical journal which his father had founded and of which Schnitzler was now the editor. How very differently, and how wittily, the topic is handled in the play.

As the curtain rises on Anatol's room, Max says to him, 'Really, Anatol, I do envy you', to which the casual hero's only response is a smile. Anatol is in love again, but has doubts about 'her' true feelings towards him. Very soon, but very gradually, a theme is introduced which will serve as a unifying element all through the cycle: Anatol would love to know the truth, yet he knows that in affairs of the heart it is always elusive: 'If I were to fall on my knees before her and say, "Darling, you're forgiven in advance, but do please tell me the truth!" – what good would that do me?' This theme – the pursuit and evasion of truth – recurs time and again throughout the cycle, varied constantly by the addition of other topics all of which seemed to Schnitzler to be closely related. What, after all, is truth?

> ANATOL. If I ask her 'Do you love me?' she says 'Yes', and she's telling the truth. And when I ask her 'Are you true to me?' she says 'Yes' again, and again it's the truth, because she has totally forgotten all the others – at least for the moment.

The 'truth' theme is thus inextricably bound up with another theme which is also of central importance in Schnitzler's dramatic writing: that of the moment in time. He instinctively realised its supreme importance in relation to emotional truth and life itself, but how to convey this importance in dramatic terms provided a challenge to which much of his finest work is a response. At their best, his plays succeed in generating a sense of immediacy and spontaneity which implies that true realism resides not so much in authenticity of setting and accuracy of characterisation and detail as in a performing text's ability to evoke and communicate the unique immediacy of each vital moment in the chronological sequence of a dramatic action. Indeed, for Schnitzler the sequence of vital moments is the equivalent of conventional dramatic action. Schnitzler's concentration on the moment, on the briefest of passing episodes, in order to kindle dramatic interest was not only a challenge to actors, especially those trained in the theatrical conventions of the day; it was also a repudiation of the notion of plot, and thus of the well-made play, which was enjoying a new lease of life thanks to Ibsen and had established itself as the vehicle for social drama and for drawing-room plays of the lighter kind. This central aspect of Schnitzler's art is clearly stated in *Anatol's Megalomania* (*Anatols Größenwahn*), an eighth one-acter originally intended to provide a coda to the cycle, when Anatol, now older and maturer, observes to Max,

> Women imagine they are play-acting only because they cannot
> understand why they are now one thing, now another. Yet
> often enough there's not a trace of play-acting about it. They
> don't even tell fibs nearly as often as we men imagine . . . it's
> only that for them the truth itself is changing minute by
> minute.

A Question to Destiny, the first playlet, demonstrates
Schnitzler's ability to generate issues of genuine philosophical
and existential interest from material usually associated with
farce and boulevard comedy. Max suggests that, as Anatol is
so interested in the scientific application of hypnosis, he should
hypnotise Cora and then ask her to tell him the truth. Delighted
at the prospect of being put out of his misery and uncertainty,
Anatol accepts the idea; but Max's remark 'I'd be really curious
to know . . .' promptly raises reservations in his mind, and
heralds the emergence of another, related theme. 'I had almost
forgotten', says Max, 'that a friend's first duty is to preserve
his friend's illusions.' In Schnitzler's dramatic world, truth,
reality and the moment are henceforth to be more sharply
defined by the contrasting but equally pervasive theme of
illusion, an essentially negative concept at this early stage, since
it is what human beings cling to most of the time, whereas truth
is something they appreciate only in rare moments of insight
and emotional intensity. For its part, illusion is frequently
associated with conventional attitudes and stereotyped emotional
responses, and with that implicitly dishonest sentimentality
which marks so much of the lesser drama of the period and
represented the major obstacle to realism as Schnitzler
understood it.

Having hypnotised Cora, Anatol is given his opportunity to
discover the truth, but he finds it very hard to frame a question

which will elicit the right response, and is increasingly troubled by his growing awareness of the subconscious, that mysterious element of human personality and motivation which was being brought to public attention by contemporary medical research, especially in Vienna. Max observes that Anatol will not dare ask the fatal question, because Cora's answer might reveal that she does indeed correspond to his idea or stereotype of women, and he would a thousand times rather preserve his illusion than accept this truth. Of course Max is right. Anatol asks him to leave the room while he asks Cora the fatal question. Once alone with her, he quickly brings her round from her hypnotic trance and then, in Max's presence, maintains that she has said she truly loves him. Even Cora seems surprised to hear this. For Max, however, it seems conclusive proof that women tell lies even when under hypnosis.

Christmas Shopping takes us to an elegant shopping street in Vienna on Christmas Eve, as snow is falling. It is a delightfully well-crafted example of the conversation piece, a type of drama which anticipates the modern radio play or *Hörspiel* in its economy of means and reliance on aural effects and human voices. Anatol is helped by a lady friend to choose a present for a female acquaintance of rather different social background: what they do not say to each other in the process should, in good performance, be as audible as the actual platitudes they utter.

In *Episode* Anatol's efforts to dispose of the past and all reminders of it coincides with the return to Vienna of Bianca, an actress better known to her friends as Bibi. He reminisces to Max about the women in his life – especially Bianca; but when she turns up on Max's invitation, her recollections of Anatol seem decidedly vaguer. As she tells Max, 'One cannot remember everything' – an attitude which makes ironic fun of Anatol's nostalgia for past moments and calls into question both his sentimental illusions and the nature of emotional truth.

The theme of remembrance of things past links *Episode* with the next playlet, *Mementoes*, which did not figure in the first complete productions of *Anatol* in Vienna and Berlin in 1910, and was not performed till 1916. On the eve of his wedding to Emilie, Anatol discovers that she has not quite managed to obliterate her past. The scene is her room: it is an autumn evening, and through the open window a tree may be seen, its leaves nearly all fallen. She makes a good case for herself: the man she first loved and the day she first loved him are of abiding value to her because, as she says, 'one must have learnt how to love in order to be able to love as I love you'. At his male inability to accept such excuses she exclaims, 'You just can't take the truth, can you!' At this, Anatol is humbled, and Emilie seems to have got the better of him. In a moment of rare tenderness, she volunteers to throw away the offending ruby (one of the 'mementoes' of the title) – though not the black diamond, because that is worth a quarter of a million. Such mercenariness is too much for Anatol. He flings the jewel into the fireplace. As Emilie attempts to rescue it with a pair of tongs, he leaves the room with the calmly uttered insult, 'Dirne!' ('You slut!').

The interplay of past and present is vividly brought out in the next playlet, *A Farewell Supper*, in which Anatol's carefully staged parting with Annie is comically and ironically upstaged by Annie's choice of that very same occasion to tell him that her affair with him is over. In this deftly-turned light comedy, the action is as amusing as the words. The opening exchanges between Max and Anatol have much in common with those between Jack and Algernon in *The Importance of Being Earnest* (1895); both are unmistakably products of the 1890s, but theatrically speaking there is a great gulf between Wilde's elaborate, well-made social comedy and Schnitzler's string of episodic, impressionistic sketches.

Death Pangs (*Agonie*), the least known of the Anatol plays, is in some ways the richest and most rewarding. A sensitive study of the death-throes of a love affair, it is also a study in passing moods. At such times there are moments when everything is lovelier than ever before; never do we experience a greater longing for happiness, Anatol realises, than during these last, lingering days of love. During the course of the action, such as it is, the stage-directions specify that dusk is slowly falling; the lighting is in perfect harmony with the elegiac mood of the piece, its preoccupation with the inextricable web of past, present and future, with fading, withering and dying – moods and metamorphoses which Schnitzler was later to explore in greater depth in his masterpiece in this vein, *The Lonely Way* (1904). The practical approach to love-making demonstrated by Else, Anatol's married mistress in this episode, comes as something of a blunt anti-climax, but its irony is refreshing: for a moment Anatol was in danger of sentimental self-indulgence, and was almost taken in by the haunting atmosphere his author had created.

Anatol's Wedding Morning (*Anatols Hochzeitsmorgen*) was intended as a finale to the cycle, which by now can clearly be seen to have similarities to the musical suite or serenade scored for small ensemble, a genre which was being cultivated by Austrian composers of the period, such as Schnitzler's Viennese contemporaries Richard Heuberger and Robert Fuchs. It really seems that Anatol's amorous career has come to a happy end. His wedding is to take place shortly, and the presence in his bedroom off stage of an actress called Ilona (the set anticipates the fourth scene of *The Round Dance*) is something of an embarrassment as the happy time draws near. How is he to dispose of her, the last in a long line? As he gets into his morning clothes Anatol gradually breaks the news to Ilona, leaving it to his friend Max to console her by pointing out that it is always possible that Anatol may come back to her: at least she will never be his betrayed wife. 'Auf Wiedersehen,' says Ilona; her ambiguous curtain line, which may not be a last goodbye, makes it clear that this is a false ending, and that the whole sequence or cycle could start all over again – an idea which Schnitzler was to follow up and develop in *The Round Dance*, which *Anatol* foreshadows in so many ways.

'Liebelei'

Anatol was followed by *Liebelei*, a shortish play in three acts. At its first performance at the Burgtheater on 9 October 1895 it was coupled with a German version of a short play by Giuseppe Giacosa, the leading Italian dramatist of the day, best known for his three-act play *Tristi amori* (*Sad loves*, 1887). *Liebelei* (or *Dalliance*, as Tom Stoppard's version is called) is the nearest Schnitzler comes to the type of topical realistic play which was proving so successful in the hands of his European contemporaries, plays which create their dramatic effect from observation of the conflict between the emotional needs of individuals and the claims of society as embodied in its conventions and institutions – marriage, the family, codes of honour and professional ethics. Here, a young and obviously well-heeled man-about-town, Fritz Lobheimer, encounters a young woman of socially inferior status, Christine Weiring, and inspires in her, tragically, the great love of her life.

The stage-settings reflect the divisions which their relationship cannot transcend. Act I takes place in Fritz's rooms, where the emphasis is all on casual elegance and comfort; Acts II and III are contrastingly set in Christine's home, described as '*nice and unassuming*'. But the human set-up is not quite so simple. The social and financial imbalance between the two lovers is compensated for by a distinct cultural advantage on the girl's side, which acts as a contributory factor to the drama. Christine's father plays the violin in the orchestra of a Viennese theatre, and what she lacks in social graces she makes up for in general culture. When Fritz visits her in Act II he at first declares that her room is exactly as he expected it to be; closer scrutiny, however, reveals details which do not fit into his conventional picture. She possesses books (the works of Schiller and Hauff, and even an encyclopaedia) and on the stove there is a bust of someone whom rich young Fritz does not recognise: the composer Franz Schubert, a figure whose physiognomy is familiar enough to all German-speakers with any pretensions to culture. Thus the playwright establishes the ambience of his characters, and gives his contemporary German and Austrian audiences their cultural bearings: the tragic nobility of self-sacrifice symbolised by Schiller; a certain rather old-fashioned romantic strain associated with Hauff; and an instinctive responsiveness to words and to the lyrical dimensions of a moment, such as marks Schubert's songs – all these are facets of Christine's personality reflected in her personal possessions, in stage-properties which are therefore of essential importance. Dormant till now, these traits will be kindled into life through Christine's relationship with Fritz. Not only will his charm and friendliness generate love; his shallowness and casualness in affairs of the heart will cause her to overcompensate, and to romanticise and idealise their pleasant little flirtation until it assumes the pathos of a tragic novelette.

Her father tries to put her on her guard. In Act III there is a dialogue of great sensitivity and subtlety reminiscent of the great father-daughter duets in Verdi operas:

WEIRING. A young fellow like that – what can he know? Has he the least idea of what has fallen into his lap? Can he possibly tell the difference between what is genuine and what isn't? And as for all this foolish love of yours – did he ever really know what that was all about?

CHRISTINE (*with mounting anxiety*). You haven't...you didn't go and see him?

WEIRING. Whatever makes you think that? He's away, isn't he?

It all comes too late, because young Fritz is already dead and buried, killed in a duel by the husband of a lady with whom he has been having an affair. When she learns what has happened, Christine draws her conclusions:

I was no more to him than a nice way of passing the time – and he died for the sake of somebody else...! And yet I worshipped him; didn't he even realise? Didn't he know that I gave him absolutely everything I had, that I would willingly have died for him, that he was my God and my salvation? Did it really never cross his mind?

Her impulse in this mood of despair is to go to his graveside and join him in death. There is little the others – her elderly father or her friend Mizi – can do, because Christine is set on a course which is totally in keeping with her character and a manifestation of her urge for romantic wish-fulfilment, even in death. She would rather die than accept the world as it is and men as they are. The scepticism that would otherwise inevitably ensue is typical of many other characters in Schnitzler plays. In a way, the impulsive, generous-hearted young heroine of *Liebelei* is a throwback from the hard-bitten, sophisticated world of Schnitzler's Vienna to an earlier period; it is no coincidence that the works of Schiller catch Fritz's attention in her chaste and modest home, for her personality, her social station and her tragedy all echo those of Luise Miller, her prototype in Schiller's own youthful domestic tragedy *Kabale und Liebe* (*Intrigue and Love*, 1784). Like Christine, Schiller's Luise is a musician's daughter, though she is also the heroine

126

of a tragic opera modelled by Verdi on Schiller's play. *Liebelei*, coming as it does between Schnitzler's pioneering early plays *Anatol* and *The Round Dance*, is a reminder that even the most forward-looking playwrights have traditions behind them.

In Otto Erich Hartleben's *Rosenmontag* (1900), a popular German play of the same period, Hans Rudorff, a young Prussian officer, finds himself unable to get over a love affair with a girl who is socially unacceptable to his class and family: though typical enough of his social background and by no means a misfit, he cannot resist the urge to see the girl once more, and in order to do so breaks his word of honour to his commanding officer. The professional and social consequences of this action are clear-cut: recognising them, he shoots himself and the girl. Seen in the light of this fine play and others like it, such as Sudermann's great box-office success of 1890, *Honour* (*Die Ehre*), Schnitzler's *Liebelei* assumes even greater interest and complexity, and shows clearly the direction in which his writing was going. It is easy enough to dismiss Fritz as a casual, rich young man with little or no depth to his personality, and to let all our sympathies be drawn to Christine, vulnerable, loving, and so obviously his uncomprehending 'victim'. But is this a reading borne out by the text, and, more especially, by what lies between the lines? There are clues pointing towards a different interpretation. These are mainly located in the first act, in the course of which Fritz and his pal Theodor entertain the two girls, Christine and Mizi, to supper. The evening is delightful, but very early on Christine is troubled by Fritz's mood, which he says reflects the fact that he may need to go away for a long time. In any case, he adds, they may have seen enough of each other already. Her response to this – 'I would never want to leave you as long as I live: I love you' – naturally prejudices the audience in her favour and against him, especially given his reply: 'Please don't say things like that. I don't like big words. Let's not talk about eternity.' It is not until later that we discover the fate hanging over Fritz, and by then his debonair manner and the brave face he puts on it make it hard for us to reconcile ourselves to the fact that this pleasant, ordinary young man is marked by death. This theme recurs in Act II when Fritz pays his first and last visit to Christine in her home:

FRITZ. Why are you so often unhappy?
CHRISTINE. Because I long for you so; when you aren't here with me, it's as though you weren't even in the same city. It's as though you were somewhere quite different...as though you had gone out of my life, far far away.

To such words, from the girl he will probably never see again, Fritz replies,

Come here, come to me...you know, as I do, that at this moment you love me. Don't talk about 'for ever'. (*Almost to himself*) Maybe there are moments which do radiate an aura of eternity... That is the only kind of eternity we can ever understand, and the only kind that can ever be ours.... (*He kisses her – pause – then exclaims*) Oh, how wonderful it is to be with you!

It becomes evident here that the supreme experience an ordinary mortal can have is his, rather than hers. She loves wholeheartedly, romantically, uncomprehendingly. His love for her achieves fulfilment when the sight and the sound and the presence of her enable him to transcend his own impending extinction by affirming life and holding self-pity at bay. After *Anatol* and its irredeemably self-centred protagonist, Schnitzler's depiction of Fritz in *Liebelei* takes on greater significance. The plot of the play may be reminiscent of a dramatised novelette of the period, but its tragic impact is devoid of both cynicism and sentimentality. Its salvation lies in its irony and the author's skill in placing its key utterances at points in the action where their full significance is played down and can easily be missed by the first-time reader or the audience at a second-rate performance. There is no need to play the *dénouement* out to the accompaniment of an on-stage rehearsal of a sugary Viennese operetta, as happens in *Dalliance*, Tom Stoppard's version of *Liebelei*, which was staged by the National Theatre, London, in 1986. Over-emphasis is out of place in Schnitzler.

'The Round Dance'

At first, *The Round Dance* (*Reigen*) appears to be an extension of *Anatol* – a sequence of episodic playlets highlighting a variety of amorous relationships, yet unified by recurrent themes. But though there are undeniable similarities in format and conception, *The Round Dance* represents a radical new departure in two respects. Its presentation of character moves away from the realistic portrayal of rounded individuals, such as Christine and Fritz or Anatol and his lady-friends, in favour of a detached, impersonal approach. The characters are presented as types – the young man, the maid, and so on – in a way which anticipates the manner of German Expressionism. But though *The Round Dance* registers a move towards Expressionist techniques in character presentation, the dialogue itself tends in a different direction. Instead of the repartee, the *bons mots*, and the generally 'scripted' sophistication of the Anatol cycle, the dialogue in *The Round Dance* moves much closer to the all-out Naturalism which writers, especially in Berlin, had been developing for the stage. What the characters say to one another is recorded, as it were, from life, with all its inconsistencies, repetitions, corrections, false starts, and other subtler but equally significant paralinguistic signals. Dialogue is now the natural expression of the relatively mindless verbal exchanges that preface and follow the sex-act itself.

The idea was a good one: one wonders why no one had thought of it before. Perhaps someone had, but it was of course unthinkable on the modern stage until in the Vienna of the early 1900s a sufficiently large group of open-minded theatre-goers, a good many of them members of the medical profession, were able to provide a potential audience in sympathy with what Schnitzler was doing and the encouragement he needed to bring out into the open what he had in mind. For centuries European drama – both tragedy and comedy–had turned on the theme of love. Now, while in Paris Feydeau was exploring the comic dramatic potential of 'animal instincts', Schnitzler was asking audiences in Vienna to face up to the well-known fact that, by and large, 'love' is a synonym or, rather, a euphemism for sex. He displayed his mounting confidence as a writer for the theatre by making the sex-act (discreetly assigned to the wings in his previous plays) into the central event of each of the ten self-contained scenes of *The Round Dance*: sex is their unifying factor.

It was a brilliant stroke to make the opening scene an encounter between a prostitute and a soldier; straightaway the central theme is presented in its most basic, uncomplicated form, devoid as yet of the accretions of civilised conduct, social convention and small talk under which it is generally hidden. Schnitzler was drawing the logical literary consequences from the biological and sociological discoveries of the late nineteenth century: sex is the basic manifestation of life, and he therefore presents it as the common denominator of a wide cross-section of humanity drawn from the widely differing social strata of Viennese society. Beginning at the lowest end of the social scale, the ten scenes of which the play is made up take us into the solid *haute-bourgeoisie* of the city and beyond, into the élites of the artistic world and the aristocracy, before bringing us back again, full circle, to the prostitute of the opening scene, who had solicited a soldier, who then seduced a chambermaid who in her turn seduces the son of her well-to-do employers; he then seduces a young, newly-married lady, she her own husband, he a sweet young thing, she a dramatic poet, he the actress he hopes will create his newest role, and she an aristocratic army captain, who in the final scene wakes up at six in the morning to find himself, fully clothed, on a divan in the prostitute's shabby room. Justifying the drama's title, the action has come back to where it started, and done so with comic *élan* and formal elegance. Casual and irresponsible though its incidents of loving and love-making are – and they are at their most false and shallow in the scene where the self-indulgent poet courts the calculating actress – one comes away from *The Round Dance* with a sense of satisfaction which outweighs any feeling of disgust and disappointment at so ignoble a portrayal of human behaviour. At the very least, it is a *tour de force* of comic invention. And there are tinges of pathos amidst the laughter.

The Round Dance is a play without a moral, and Schnitzler maintained that he never intended it for the theatre. This, as much as the 'naughty' nature of its subject matter, was responsible for the long postponement of its first public production. The play was written during the winter of 1896-7; a limited private edition followed in 1900, and the text was on sale to the general public in 1903; however, the first public performance did not take place until 23 December 1920, in Berlin, where it was directed by Gertrud Eysoldt, who had made her name as Wedekind's Lulu. In the next few weeks it was also staged in Hamburg, Munich and Leipzig, but it soon aroused vociferous and violent opposition on the grounds of gross indecency. Attempts were made to interfere with performances in Berlin. In Vienna, the first production at the Volkstheater, which opened on 1 February 1921, was halted in the midst of a scandal which assumed national proportions and threatened to develop political dimensions. Back in Berlin, a court case was brought, but ended in the acquittal of Gertrud Eysoldt and all her actors.

In defence of the play, Schnitzler smilingly pointed out that in some of the best dramas the curtain falls as the lovers embrace; the trouble in *The Round Dance* is that they go on talking after the curtain has fallen or the lights have gone down, or after the row of dashes which, in the printed text, draws the reader's attention to the omission of the central 'action' of each scene. That, said Schnitzler, is the fun of it; or, to put it another way, the 'moral' of the story is that life goes on. This basic tenet of Naturalist drama, which had already called into question the credibility of conventional nineteenth-century *dénouements*, applies to *The Round Dance* too. But, with characteristic originality, Schnitzler adheres to it in the context of the bedroom rather than the death-bed. If more serious notes are sounded, they are unobtrusive, and scarcely more than stock symptoms of post-coital depression.

Attempts to make out that *The Round Dance* is darker and, by implication, deeper, a dance of death rather than a lively roundelay, suggest a wish on the part of critics and producers to find a moral framework for Schnitzler's play without a moral. There is scant evidence in the text to suggest that the spectre of mortality is waiting in the wings, or to substantiate the notion that, since it was written by a qualified physician, it may really be an allegory on the transmission of venereal disease, which notoriously knows no boundaries of social class, may be regarded as the wages of sin, and was certainly widespread in Vienna.

This embarrassing subject had surfaced in late-nineteenth-century dramatic literature with Ibsen's *Ghosts* (1881), and it gained further notoriety with *Damaged Goods* (*Les Avariés*, 1901), by the controversial French playwright

Eugène Brieux. But, unlike Ibsen and Brieux, Schnitzler was not writing a problem-play. Herbert Jhering, the distinguished German drama critic, was much nearer the mark when, in his review of the first performance, he remarked that '*The Round Dance* is unproblematical, and will probably become a classic of German erotic literature, an area in which we are badly off.' Equally apt was his comment that a later writer writing a play which centred entirely on the sex-act would do so differently, and also more crudely.

The Round Dance is a play which needs plenty of tact, as Max Reinhardt was the first to point out; if the subtle inflections of Viennese speech and the details of Viennese manners are not captured, the true qualities of the text are apt to evaporate, and we are left with an episodic and rather smutty entertainment in which Schnitzler's delightfully varied and pointed dialogue might just as well be replaced by coarse innuendo and heavy breathing.

The problems *The Round Dance* poses for non-Austrian actors and producers became evident in the play's first major production at the Royal Exchange Theatre, Manchester on 1 January 1982. Instead of attempting an authentic evocation of Viennese life at the turn of the century – which in the original is largely conveyed through Schnitzler's use of language – the production (played in an adapted version of a translation by Charles Osborne) salvaged as much as it could of Schnitzler's comedy of situation, re-creating it in a setting and ambience audibly and visibly nearer to the popular Manchester-based television soap-opera *Coronation Street* than to imperial Vienna. The result might have been written by a northern Pinero in a moment of furtive abandon; the play was there, but not Schnitzler's lost world. Yet it worked, and showed that Schnitzler's masterpiece can be translated to different social and linguistic environments without losing its laughs or its pathos.

The one-act plays

During the 1890s Schnitzler wrote a number of other full-length plays which were performed with more or less success at the time, but which have not proved so durable. *Free Game* (*Freiwild*, 1896) and *The Legacy* (*Das Vermächtnis*, 1898), both premièred in Berlin, are three-act problem-plays and have many features in common with other examples of this genre, which was enjoying international popularity at the turn of the century. *Free Game* castigates the mindless arrogance of the Austrian officer class and the tendency of its members to regard attractive young actresses as 'fair game': it is a play with overt satirical force. *The Legacy* takes the lid off the upper middle class's most cherished proprieties when the critically injured son of a respectable family confesses to his mother that he is the father of an illegitimate child, hoping that she will look after it and its mother after he is gone. In the latter play especially, Schnitzler's craftmanship cannot quite persuade the spectator that the foreseeable outcome is really a surprise logically motivated by the interplay of his characters' personalities and social attitudes.

Alongside these full-length plays, he devoted much time to that favourite genre of his, the one-acter, which was also enjoying something of a vogue at the time. The fading and passing of love is the favourite subject of his early one-act plays. *Half-past One* (*Halbzwei*, 1894), a dialogue between lovers in the small hours, anticipated *The Round Dance* by showing how passion or love fades away once the sexual urge has been gratified. In *The Hysterical Person* (*Die überspannte Person*, 1894), love fades and passes as a woman tells her lover that she is expecting his child; he advises her to resume sexual relations with her husband forthwith, a suggestion which, coming from him, appals and disillusions her. Neither of these two short plays, with their stark revelations, was performed until

1932, but in 1899 the Burgtheater put on *The Companion* (*Die Gefährtin*) along with Schnitzler's most ambitious shorter play, *The Green Cockatoo* (*Der grüne Kakadu*). *The Companion* is another play with similarities to *The Round Dance*. A professor of medicine discovers on the very day of the funeral of his unfaithful wife that her lover, an assistant of his whose unlawful relationship to her he had broadmindedly condoned, had in fact been untrue to her in his turn and, worse still, that his wife had broadmindedly condoned this. The darker colouring of this play also marks two of the one-acters in the set *Living Hours* (*Lebendige Stunden*), performed in Berlin in 1902 and in Vienna the year after. In the title piece a terminally ill mother commits suicide so as not to be a burden to her son, who is a gifted writer: it is a sacrifice which he accepts (much to the annoyance of the great Austrian poet Rainer Maria Rilke, who felt that the cap fitted!). In *Last Masks* (*Die letzten Masken*) Schnitzler's growing preoccupation with the theme of dying fuses nicely with his earlier, light-hearted 'naughty' manner as a dying journalist reveals that a successful writer was all the time being deceived by his very own wife.

Schnitzler achieved near-perfection in many of his one-act plays. His strengths are particularly evident in those cast in the form of duologues; here his ability to bring individual characters to life through the closest possible attention to the tell-tale rhythms and nuances of speech, its shifting pace and even its omissions, indicates that, if the medium of the radio play had existed in his lifetime, he would have been one of its finest exponents.

One of the very best of his one-acters, and one which comes very close to the spirit of the radio play (as opposed to the radio dramatisation), is *Literature* (*Literatur*), the fourth of the *Living Hours* quartet. *Literature* is a conversation piece scored for three voices; its shape is the eternal triangle and its theme that perennial post-Romantic problem, the relationship of life to literature. The dialogues between the three voices – a duet for Klemens and Margarete, another for Margarete and Gilbert, and a concluding trio – explore this theme with such subtlety and sophistication that, jejune though it is, new light is unexpectedly shed on it from a variety of angles. Klemens is a debonair young aristocrat, a man-about-town with a passion for horses, whose intention it is to settle down and marry Margarete, a young *divorcée* who is managing remarkably well to adapt to his tastes or at least adopt his jargon. Margarete is under no misapprehensions about herself: 'I'm just a very complex person,' she tells her fiancé. She is in fact a woman with a past – an artistic past. She had consoled herself for her marital problems (her husband was a rich but stout cotton manufacturer) by consorting with artists and writers in Munich (some of them Jewish, like Schnitzler) and writing poetry herself. Fortunately, however, she has now given all this up – or has she? Klemens, whose interest in art and poetry is minimal, has a shock when she reveals that she has written a novel and that it is already in the publisher's hands. Such news is too much for him: exit Klemens. Enter Gilbert, one of Margarete's friends from her literary past. It is just a polite call to say hello; but before they know where are are they have picked up the pieces and are engaged in 'literary' conversation from which it emerges that the lovely poems she had addressed to him as her 'slender, fair-locked lover' were not really inspired by him at all but were 'just' literature. He, however, being a 'true' artist, has transmuted their mutual experiences into the art-form of a novel. But so, she says, has she.

This confession brings them very close again; but curiosity soon gets the better of Gilbert. How close to real life is her novel? She explains that all the events and characters in it have been disguised (for instance, in it she deceives her husband with a baritone, not a tenor . . .); indeed Gilbert would find difficulty in recognising himself were it not for the fact that she has incorporated all their love-letters. The trouble is, so has he, in his: each had taken care to keep a copy of their spontaneous and intimate effusions. Surely they are ideally suited to each other? This happy outcome is prevented by Klemens's return. Fortunately, amongst these people passion and panic promptly give way to polite conversation. They talk about Gilbert's new novel and about how he drew inspiration for it from his own experience. Realising that Klemens has seen through him and knows a great deal more about their past than he lets on, Gilbert hands over the manuscript:

KLEMENS. How kind of you. Truth to tell, German novels are not my cup of tea. Still, this is the last one I shall ever read – or rather, the last but one.

MARGARETE AND GILBERT (*together*). The last but one?

KLEMENS. Yes.

MARGARETE. So what will the last one be?

KLEMENS. Yours, my dear. (*He produces a copy of it from his pocket.*) You see, I asked the publisher to let me have a copy for you – or rather, for us both.

MARGARETE *and* GILBERT *look at each other in consternation.*

MARGARETE. How kind of you... (*Taking the novel*) Yes, it's mine all right.

KLEMENS. And we shall read it together.

MARGARETE. No, Klemens, no; I couldn't possibly ask so much of you. (*Throwing the book into the open fire*) I don't want to hear anything about it, ever again.

GILBERT (*with joyful relief*). But, gnädige Frau!...

KLEMENS (*stepping towards the fireplace*). What on earth are you doing?

MARGARETE (*standing in front of the fireplace and holding out her arms to embrace Klemens*). Now will you believe that I really love you?

GILBERT (*delighted*). It seems I'm *de trop*. Gnädige Frau,
Herr Baron.... (*Aside*) Why did I never think of that
ending?

The coincidence here of theme (art and life, or turning one's
life into an autobiographical novel), plot (burning the
incriminating evidence) and effective curtain line ('Why did I
never think of that ending?') is a good example of Schnitzler's
deft craftsmanship. He knew how to turn out a well-made play
and had obviously perfected his art by observing the example
of the French exponents of the conversation-piece and their
German-language imitators. The wit and expertise of playlets
such as *Literature* show him to be the Viennese counterpart of
his French contemporaries such as Georges de Porto-Riche
(1849–1947) and Tristan Bernard (1866–1947).

Audiences in the era leading up to the First World War had
an enormous appetite for plays which were short, entertaining,
not too heavy, and true to life, though not depressing in the
way that Naturalist drama almost inevitably was. Schnitzler was
only one of many authors who provided the theatres with such
plays. What distinguishes his shorter plays, apart from their
uniquely Viennese flavour, is the delicate balance they achieve
between the trivial and the tragic. Beneath the surface of their
superficial dialogue there is an underlying sense of truth, for
Schnitzler was unusual in being able to accept that for shallow,
superficial people the truth is not always very profound. No
doubt he was aware that many people in the audience would
be limited in this way; indeed, his plays reflect the proportions
he observed in real life of superficiality to profundity, sincerity
to falsehood, comedy to tragedy, the bitter to the sweet. Anyone
can appreciate *Literature*, even people like Klemens who enjoy
plays but do not appreciate literature. On one level *Literature*
is a skit on self-indulgent 'literary' attitudes, yet on another it
is a penetrating analysis of people's differing perceptions of how

life relates to literature, an analysis conducted with enough subtlety and insight to justify its being called 'literature' in its own right, and obviously drawing on its author's personal experience. In other words, the appeal of *Literature* extends from the most illiterate person in the audience to the most cultured and sophisticated, and in doing so reflects the composition of the theatre-going public of the period in which Schnitzler was working. *Literature* is a delicious example of Schnitzler's genius for concision and economy. But he could also develop the one-act form into drama of more ample dimensions.

If *Literature* is a light-hearted trio, *Countess Mitzi, or The Family Reunion* (*Comtesse Mitzi, oder Der Familientag*), first performed at the Deutsches Volkstheater in Vienna on 5 January 1909, could be called a mellow, warm-hearted quartet with astringent passages. It is essentially a conversation-piece for four voices set in the garden of a small eighteenth-century country house somewhere outside Vienna – the sort of setting in which the chamber music of Haydn and Mozart would be at home. The play treats a familiar subject, family reunion; but this time the result is an amusing burlesque. The moment has come for the Count, Mitzi's elderly father, to bid farewell to Lollo, his long-time mistress, who has decided that the time is ripe for her to quit the stage and seek respectability in a middle-class marriage; the time has also come for Egon, the Count's old friend, to introduce to them his hitherto discreetly hidden natural son, whom he has decided to adopt and who will inherit his title. The Count's daughter, Mitzi, is an attractive spinster of thirty-seven and of course she knows nothing whatsoever about all these matters: after all, they lie well outside the bounds of a well-brought-up young lady's knowledge or awareness. But the truth, as we gradually discover, is otherwise. For most of her life Mitzi has known about her widowed father's liaison with Lollo and happily tolerated it; nor does the unexpected appearance of Egon's boy, a perky seventeen-year-old, give her as much surprise as it does her father. After all, though her father was too taken up with his own love-life at the time to notice, it was she that gave him birth! It might appear that this double-stranded plot has plenty of potential human anguish below its surface; perhaps it has, but these people are all too civilised and good-natured to indulge in double tragedies. As young Philip puts it when brought into what is rather more his family than he realises, 'Happy families depend on everyone getting on well together.' At the end of the play, the prospect of them all meeting up at the seaside in Ostend suggests the possibility of a happy future.

Countess Mitzi may have lost some of its original appeal and strike modern play-goers or readers as lightweight by comparison with plays such as *The Round Dance* or *The Vast Domain*. But its lightness is its abiding quality. The cruder but fleeting encounters of sex are left well behind; what endures are relationships founded neither on truth nor on passing fancy, the relationships of people who may on occasion be malicious and dishonest, but who are tolerant and mellow enough to know that truth is not necessarily an end in itself, and that it is often wiser and better for all concerned to accept this knowledge silently and go on living.

The Green Cockatoo shows a totally different side of Schnitzler the dramatist; it takes its name from a low tavern in Paris where people gather on the eve of the French Revolution. It is not surprising that this 'dramatic grotesque', as Schnitzler called it, aroused the objections of an Austrian archduchess and had to be taken off after eight performances when Paul Schlenther first staged it at the Vienna Burgtheater in 1899; initially it was also banned in Berlin. It remains a very disturbing theatrical experience. As the crowds gather off stage to storm the Bastille, the landlord, a former theatre manager, and his troupe of out-of-work actors entertain decadent pleasure-

seeking aristocrats to an extempore enactment of revolution
which takes on something of the urgency of what is really
occurring outside as it degenerates into mounting confusion.
The play within the play takes on such a life of its own that
it casts doubt on the 'reality' that surrounds it and which is
guaranteed for the audience by its specific and familiar historical
setting. It achieves this effect thanks largely to the central
character of the actor Henri (a role associated particularly with
Josef Kainz), whose farewell performance we and the aristocrats
are supposed to be watching; Henri assumes the role of a
deceived husband while, in reality, his pretty wife is deceiving
him with a duke. As he inveighs against the privileged and
dissolute nobleman, everyone assumes he is play-acting, so that,
when it occurs, his murder of the duke seems so 'in character'
and so obviously part of the play being extemporised that it
cannot be taken seriously. Where, then, does make-believe end
and reality begin? Are we not all playing roles which ring true
only now and then? These are the questions which this brilliant
one-act play poses and which it answers strictly in terms of
theatre; in doing so it brings to the surface the deepest anxieties
of a society in decay and exorcises them by a dazzling exercise
in dramatic irony which reaches its ultimate twist after the final
curtain as we, the audience, emerge into the 'real' world and
have to face the fact that what we have just witnessed was no
more, and no less, than a play conceived by Schnitzler at the
height of his powers.

'The Lonely Way'

The *joie de vivre* of Schnitzler's best-known plays is offset by
darker visions. To see him as a purveyor of Viennese charm
is justifiable up to a point: he had an appealing gift for erotic
comedy and could capture in words the sentimental, smiling,

wistful lilt of a Viennese waltz. But this applies only to certain areas of Schnitzler's theatre. From early on in his career, he was also acutely aware of disease and death. As early as 1880 he was expressing a wish to immerse himself in the thought of death while still happily glowing with the mad whirl of life. If his affairs with the actresses Mizi Glümer and Adele Sandrock provided ample subject matter for one aspect of his drama (and they were the prototypes of some of his most successful female characters), his love for the singers Marie Reinhard and Olga Gussman provided emotional insights of a deeper sort. The sardonic little comedy *The Lady with the Dagger* (*Die Frau mit dem Dolche*, 1901) shows a writer turning his wife's infidelities into plays, but Marie's death in 1899, and that of his close friend Olga Waissnix in 1897, brought home the inevitability of death, a theme that was to become the central idea of *The Lonely Way* (*Der einsame Weg*), a five-act play first performed at the Deutsches Theater, Berlin, on 13 February 1904.

Schnitzler wrote *The Lonely Way* in answer, as it were, to Hauptmann's *Lonely Lives* (*Einsame Menschen*). In it he expressed his own personal sense of loneliness and loss, blending it with an autumnal colouring which creates an apt mood for what is in effect a sequence of conversations conducted in permutation by a set of characters each of whom is in his or her way acutely conscious of the passing of the years or under the shadow of death: indeed, Stephan von Sala, the play's central character, is literally a dying man experiencing a brief encounter which may well also be the great love of his life. Little by little, but with steady inevitability, the main characters begin to reveal cracks in their healthy self-assertiveness and emotional self-centredness as they try to glean what echoes and tokens of affection they can, in the hope of counteracting, if not drowning, the 'feeling of being alone, and of being left all alone'.

Much of the plot is taken up with revelations about their various pasts; in Ibsen fashion, skeletons are let out of cupboards, as when Irene, an actress no longer young, discovers that her former lover, Julian, actually fathered a son at the time when their great love affair was at its height – but with another woman, whose death early in the play seems to him to indicate that the time has at last come to reveal the truth to the lad. Young Felix, however, decides that he will continue to regard as his true father the man who actually loved his mother. All must go their separate ways: Sala to certain death; Johanna, who loves him, to suicide; Julian and Irene towards a lonely old age; while young Felix sets off on an expedition to far-distant places. It is too late to make amends. Emotions well up and die again as this group of interlinked people disintegrates; the leaves on the trees turn reddish-brown, and darkness falls. 'Shall I put on the light?' says Julian. 'It's quite cosy in the twilight,' Irene replies.

There may be echoes of Ibsen, and similarities at times to Chekhov – Schnitzler's play dates from the same year as *The Cherry Orchard*. But *The Lonely Way* is most notable as a sensitive evocation of the atmosphere that pervaded *fin-de-siècle* Austria in the years which led up to the First World War and the end of the Austro-Hungarian Empire. Indeed, it has been seen as a kind of benign diagnosis of the ills from which that doomed society was suffering, though there is hardly a trace in it of political comment, let alone prophetic foreboding. Nowadays it is only rarely staged, even in Vienna, but when it is, it tends to be hailed by critics and audiences as one of Schnitzler's supreme achievements.

'The Vast Domain'

By his fiftieth birthday, in 1912, Schnitzler, like Hauptmann, was at the height of his fame in the German-speaking countries; in that year twenty-six of his plays were staged, three of them

143

running simultaneously in Vienna itself. On 14 October in the previous year, the second great play of his middle period, *The Vast Domain* (*Das weite Land*), was premièred in nine cities: Berlin, Breslau, Bochum, Hamburg, Hanover, Leipzig, Munich, Prague and Vienna. *The Vast Domain* marks a high point in German-language social drama on the grand scale comparable only to Hauptmann's *Before Sunset* (1932), and on the German-speaking stage it is still amongst the most popular Schnitzler plays, although outside Austria it has fared less well. In 1979 Maria Schell appeared in an acclaimed production of the play at the Salzburg Festival, and the same year saw a remarkably sensitive English version by Tom Stoppard at the National Theatre, London, under the title *Undiscovered Country*, with Dorothy Tutin as Genia and John Wood as her husband, Herr Hofreiter.

Schnitzler described *The Vast Domain* as a stylised re-creation of observed social reality, and felt that in it he had surpassed himself. It is certainly true that the thematically related plays he had written already, *Intermezzo* (*Zwischenspiel*, 1905) and *The Call of Life* (*Der Ruf des Lebens*, 1906), lack its precision and its conviction, and lapse too easily into archly knowing exchanges and melodramatic cliché. With *The Vast Domain* he recovered his touch. Subtitled 'a tragi-comedy', the play is poised between the suppressed pathos of potential tragedy and the ebullience of high social comedy, with a tinge of satire. During its five acts a net of sorts closes in on Herr Hofreiter, a successful, self-made, self-centred businessman whose easy-going life-style runs up against what may be just a conventional obstacle, but may also be part of a manifestation, in modern form, of ancient atavistic instincts and responses.

Herr Hofreiter had always assumed quite naturally that his lovely wife, Genia, was above reproach; the discovery that his assumption may be false comes as something of a relief to him, since it clearly makes his own amorous escapades and infidelities seem more forgivable. Double standards, after all, were the order of the day, and in Schnitzler's Vienna there was a relative lack of the moral rectitude that characterises Victorian respectability in Britain and the United States. When in Act IV Dr Maurer, the family doctor, implies criticism of their conduct, Genia Hofreiter disarmingly takes him to task:

> Don't take it so much to heart! How silly it would be if, with all your knowledge of the really serious aspects of life, you were to take all this playing about, this play-acting, seriously. And that is all that love affairs are, believe me, doctor. Indeed, one reaches a stage when it's all very amusing to watch and indeed to take part in.

But, counters Maurer, lies are the worst thing. Lies? she replies; are there such things when it's all only a game? They're all part of the fun! – and so they are, amongst these delightful, easy-going, well-to-do people; that is, until things get out of hand. Then social conventions come into play, for order must be maintained: it alone can make civilised coexistence possible and ease us over the chasms of embarrassment, jealousy and recrimination that can so easily open up in times of stress, as when Otto von Aigner, a young naval officer, becomes Genia's lover and her husband not only knows it (which wouldn't really matter) but knows that everybody else knows it too, which is quite intolerable. A duel ensues – this particular social convention persisted in certain Austrian circles long after it had lapsed in England – and in the duel Herr Hofreiter shoots Otto and kills him.

The obvious motive for this act is of course a noble one: an outraged husband's vindication of his family's honour in the name of order, decency and all we hold most dear. Or was it, as one young man suggests, just an act of personal retaliation? Maybe the motivation lies deeper still. As Genia and the doctor were conversing in the garden, her husband was defeating young Otto on the tennis court in a singles match; the pleasant summery sound of tennis balls can be heard off stage. But their rivalry had to be pursued still further. It had to be, says Herr Hofreiter. Had to? 'Yes, as he stood there facing me with that look of youthful insolence in his eyes, I knew it was him or me.' 'You're lying,' Genia interrupts; 'he would never have....' 'No, I'm not; you're wrong! It was a matter of life or death.' Primitive instincts surface that summer afternoon.

The build-up to these events, and the resulting disintegration of an affluent, easy-going way of life, give the play dramatic momentum, but Schnitzler's concerns are wider and deeper. In a conversation which occurs at a central point in the play, Otto's father, Dr von Aigner, a man who has cut himself off from the upper-middle-class environment he cannot stand, muses aloud to his old friend Hofreiter,

Has it never struck you what complicated creatures we humans are? There is room for so much in us: love and deceit...loyalty and disloyalty...worshipping one woman and desiring another, or indeed several others. Of course we try to keep ourselves in order as best we can, but any such order is artificial at best.... The natural state is – chaos. Yes, my dear Hofreiter, the human psyche is a vast domain, as the poet once put it.

Centrally positioned as they are, Dr von Aigner's words, with their overt reference to the title of the drama, not only point to the human need to control the complexities of psychological make-up and subconscious motivation, the workings of which were being revealed by the great Viennese psychologists of the period; they also indicate the highly developed awareness of double motivation which permeates the play, enriching its subtle textures and inviting sensitive interpretation and stage-production. For example, Herr Hofreiter's current craze is for tall, slim young women such as Erna Wahl, who stands rather outside the charmed circle whose atmosphere exerts such subtle pressures on its members. Hers is the voice, hers the actions, of forthright sincerity, at once admirable and hopelessly naïve in such knowing, sophisticated company.

The attraction between her and Hofreiter is one of opposites, even of extremes. What is not immediately evident, however, is that Erna's presence is a feature which recurs, significantly, at the end of each of the play's five acts; at the final curtain, she is left standing alone on the stage – alone to face a new world in which the conventional attitudes of the late-nineteenth-century upper middle class will no longer dictate behaviour and condition responses: a braver world in which the new individual of the twentieth century will have both the right and the chance to make free choices (indeed her name 'Wahl' means 'choice').

Was *The Vast Domain* Schnitzler's last great play, and did his era end with the First World War and the collapse of the Habsburg Empire? It did not seem so at the time. *Young Medardus (Der junge Medardus)*, a romantic fantasy set in Napoleonic times, proved very successful at least on the German-speaking stage between 1910 and 1932, and the plays he wrote during his later creative life, such as *Comedy of Seduction (Komödie der Verführung*, 1924) and *While the Summer Breezes Play (Im Spiel der Sommerlüfte*, 1929), have their admirers. However, it was his 'serious comedy' *Professor Bernhardi*, first performed in 1912 in Berlin, and banned in Austria until 1918, which has come to be regarded in a sense as the last word of a playwright who once remarked, 'As a Viennese I feel at home, but as a Jew I have never lost my sense of being an alien.'

'Professor Bernhardi'

Professor Bernhardi draws on elements from Schnitzler's medical background and professional experience, and shapes them into a drama of remorseless, almost Ibsen-like inevitability, the tone of which is lightened by comic incidents, and also deepened by an underlying sense of the fundamental dignity of human beings despite their sometimes unprepossessing exteriors and often trivial concerns. Was this the play Hauptmann was thinking of when, in 1922, he observed, 'Schnitzler should be played far more often than he is'?

There is something very close to Hauptmann's own vision of the human predicament in Schnitzler's portrayal of a respected and distinguished Jewish hospital consultant who is undermined, brought down and humiliated by jealous and hostile colleagues, who conspire to bring about his resignation. The ostensible reason behind this turn of events is his refusal to allow a Roman Catholic priest access to a dying woman on the grounds that any religious intervention might disturb her final euphoria. On one level, the play is a semi-humorous revelation of the tensions seething beneath the surface amongst the medical staff at an exclusive private clinic in Vienna; every detail rings true, and has its authentic counterpart in Schnitzler's own life and times. These tensions are generated not so much by the ethical problem posed by the Roman Catholic priest as by latent anti-semitism stimulated by the obvious success, both financial and intellectual, of Jews such as Professor Bernhardi, and by the threat he appears to pose to his less gifted colleagues and to the vested interests of the Church: Roman Catholicism was the state religion of the Austrian Empire and remained the dominant religion of the territorially smaller Austrian Republic which replaced it in 1918.

Schnitzler died on 21 October 1931. At one time *Professor Bernhardi* tended to be seen as a kind of Austrian counterpart to Shaw's *The Doctor's Dilemma* (1906), a play which had preceded Schnitzler's in its dramatisation of ethical issues in a medical context (its first German production took place in Berlin in 1908). In the light of events after Schnitzler's death, the play came to reveal deeper implications. In 1936 it seemed to some people to be a suitably topical work to put on in New York and London, where it ran at the Embassy Theatre and then at the Phoenix Theatre in a production by the author's son Heinrich Schnitzler with Leonard Sachs in the title role. By then the events it depicted and the mood it conveyed had become a vivid reflection of stark realities beginning to prevail in many parts of Europe. To this day Schnitzler's only great play to have a Jewish protagonist continues to be presented in Austria and Germany as a classic drama of extraordinary prophetic power.

The Plays in Translation

Almost all the Hauptmann plays discussed in this book exist in more or less acceptable English translations, though some are more easily available than others.

Most of his plays up to 1925 are contained in Ludwig Lewisohn's 'authorized edition' of the *Dramatic Works*, in translations by different hands: its nine volumes appeared between 1912 and 1929 (New York: B.W. Huebsch; and London: M. Secker). Some of the translations in the *Dramatic Works* had been published separately beforehand or have been reprinted since: examples are Mary Morison's fine renderings of *Lonely Lives* (1898) and *The Weavers* (1899), and Charles Henry Meltzer's dated attempts at *Hannele* (1908) and *The Sunken Bell* (1899).

More recent collections are *Five Plays*, translated by Theodore H. Lustig with an introduction by John Gassner (New York: Bantam, 1961), which includes *The Beaver Coat*, *Drayman Henschel*, *Hannele*, *Rose Bernd* and *The Weavers*; and *Gerhart Hauptmann: Three Plays*, translated by Horst Frenz and Miles Waggoner (New York: Ungar, 1951, 1980), which contains renderings into not very idiomatic English of *The Weavers*, *Hannele* and *The Beaver Coat*.

Recent translations are Peter Bauland's *Before Daybreak* (Chapel Hill: University of North Carolina Press, 1978), which tends to 'improve' on the original, and Frank Marcus's *The Weavers* (London: Methuen, 1980, 1983), a straightforward rendering with little or no attempt to convey the linguistic range of the original.

Wedekind's *Spring Awakening* can be read in two lively modern translations, one made by Tom Osborn for the Royal Court Theatre in 1963 (London: Calder and Boyars, 1969, 1977), the other by Edward Bond (London: Methuen, 1980).

The Lulu plays are available in a translation by Stephen Spender: *The Lulu Plays and Other Sex Tragedies* (London: Calder, 1977; New York: Riverrun, 1978). This collection (which also includes two minor works, *Death and Devil* and *Castle Wetterstein*) was originally published in 1952. The stage adaptation of both Lulu plays into one drama by Peter Barnes was published by Heinemann in 1971; his stage version of *The Tenor* can be found in *The Frontiers of Farce* (London: Heinemann, 1977) as *The Singer*. There is a translation of *King Nicolo; or, Such is Life* in Martin Esslin's *The Genius of the German Theater* (New York: New American Library, 1968).

Many attempts have been made to translate the famous Schnitzler plays into English. Granville Barker's stage paraphrase of *Anatol* (first published in London and New York in 1911 and reprinted several times since) remains an outstanding achievement and gives the play a convincing Edwardian flavour, while the version by Frank Marcus (London: Methuen, 1982) provides greater accuracy. A version by Charles Osborne figures in his *The Round Dance and Other*

Plays (Manchester: Carcanet, 1982), which also includes *Love Games* (*Liebelei*). Another recent version of *Liebelei*, entitled *Flirtations* (translated by Arthur S. Wensinger and Clinton J. Atkinson) is to be found in *Arthur Schnitzler: Plays and Stories*, which is vol. 55 of *The German Library* (New York: Continuum, 1982). This volume also contains *Countess Mitzi, or The Family Reunion* in a revised translation by Edwin Bjorkman, and Eric Bentley's translation of *Reigen*, here called *La Ronde*, which had previously appeared under the title *Round Dance* in Bentley's *The Classic Theater* (New York: Doubleday, 1959) and elsewhere. Another version which has made several appearances in print is by Frank and Jacqueline Marcus; most recently this has been published as *La Ronde* (London; Methuen, 1982). Carl Richard Mueller's 1967 translation has been reprinted in *An Anthology of Austrian Drama*, ed. Douglas A. Russell (East Brunswick, NJ: Farleigh Dickinson University Press, 1982) along with *The Game of Love*, his version of *Liebelei*. The stage adaptation by John Barton of Sue Davies' translation of *Reigen* has been published by Penguin (Harmondsworth, 1982) as *La Ronde*. There are at least five other English translations of this notorious play.

The Green Cockatoo can be found along with six of the *Anatol* playlets and *The Lady with the Dagger*, *Last Masks* and *Literature* from the *Living Hours* quartet in Grace Isabel Colbron's translation in *Schnitzler: One-Act Plays* (Great Neck, NY: Core, 1977). There is also an older translation in Horace B. Samuel, *The Green Cockatoo and Other Plays* (London and Edinburgh: Gay and Hancock, 1913), which also includes *The Companion* (here called *The Mate*) and *Paracelsus*. The English version of *Professor Bernhardi* used for the 1936 production was published by Victor Gollancz (London, 1936), and is also included in the same publisher's *Famous Plays of 1936*.

Tom Stoppard's *Dalliance*, his stage-version of *Liebelei*, has been published by Faber and Faber (London, 1987) in the same volume as *Undiscovered Country*, his masterly English adaptation of *Das weite Land*. While his adaptations may not always be quite accurate and may offend the purist, they succeed in capturing the essence of Schnitzler's subtle and elusive plays for today's audiences and readers.

The Personalities

A number of distinguished names associated with the Austrian and German theatre and with the plays of Hauptmann, Wedekind and Schnitzler have been mentioned in the course of this book. These brief notes are provided to help readers place them in context.

Producers

Otto Brahm (1856–1912). Academically trained critic and literary biographer, he campaigned for the new realism during the 1880s. Founder of the 'Freie Bühne' Association in Berlin, 1889–94, then director of the Deutsches Theater in Berlin, he became director of the Lessing-Theater from 1904 until his death. Germany's leading Naturalist producer, exponent of authentic milieux and situations, he saw it as his duty to allow the gifts of his actors to reveal themselves naturally and to preserve the artistic integrity of the works he produced. He was noted for the emphasis he gave to ensemble work and to the creation of a consistent atmosphere on stage. He enjoyed close working relationships with both Hauptmann and Schnitzler, but plans to direct the première of Wedekind's *Hidalla* fell through. During the legendary Brahm era some 3000 performances were given, of which 1169 were of plays by Hauptmann: in all, twenty-two Hauptmann productions were staged, of which thirteen were 'firsts'. His fifteen productions of Schnitzler were equally famous: eleven were of new plays. He also put on thirteen productions of Ibsen.

Paul Schlenther (1854–1916). Friend of Otto Brahm and dramatic critic of the Berlin liberal daily *Vossische Zeitung* from 1886 to 1898. An ardent Ibsenite, he became director of the Vienna Burgtheater in 1898 and in the same year Hauptmann's first biographer. He quarrelled with Schnitzler in the 1900–1 season with the result that Schnitzler went over to Brahm in Berlin. His wife, the actress Paula Conrad-Schlenther, created Hannele and Frau Flamm (in Hauptmann's *Rose Bernd*).

Max Reinhardt (1873–1943). Discovered by Brahm and brought to Berlin from Salzburg in Austria in 1894, he acted at the Deutsches Theater until 1902, specialising in older men and creating the role of Michael Kramer in Hauptmann's play of the same name. He then left Brahm's ensemble to take charge of the new Kleines Theater and open his own Neues Theater. He was soon Brahm's competitor in Berlin, and in 1905 took over his Deutsches Theater. He went on to become the most successful theatre producer of the period. In 1920 he founded the Salzburg Festival. He emigrated to the United States in 1933, and died in Hollywood. A brilliant producer, he stressed the visual and the evocative, and insisted on clarity of diction, even favouring the use of a chorus. A noted producer of Wedekind and Hauptmann, he never attempted Schnitzler, owing to an early misunderstanding.

Viktor Barnowsky (1875–1952). Influential Berlin director and producer at theatres such as the Kleines Theater and Lessing-Theater. Especially noted for his Wedekind.

Actresses and actors

Adele Sandrock (1864–1937). Star of the Vienna Volkstheater and of the Burgtheater. She created many major roles, including Christine in *Liebelei* and Countess Geschwitz in the first Vienna production of *Pandora's Box*. A famous Annie in Schnitzler's *Anatol* and Princess in Wedekind's *Love Potion*, she had a whirlwind romance with Schnitzler and was the original of the actress in *The Round Dance*.

Agnes Sorma (1865–1927). A classical actress who was also a noted interpreter of roles by Ibsen, Sudermann, Hauptmann and Schnitzler: she was a particularly lovely Christine in *Liebelei*. Based in Berlin and associated for a time with the Brahm ensemble, she broke away in 1897, performing in New York (Rautendelein in *The Sunken Bell*, a role she had created). She joined Max Reinhardt's ensemble in 1904. Ambitious, rich and beautiful, she became a celebrated Candida in Shaw and Mrs Alving in Ibsen's *Ghosts*. She later enjoyed a second career in films, specialising in character parts as an elderly lady.

Else Lehmann (1866–1940). The outstanding Naturalist actress in Berlin and star of the Deutsches Theater and Lessing-Theater. The epitome of the Hauptmann woman, she created Helene Krause and Rose Bernd, Frau John and Hanne Schäl. She retired from the stage after Brahm's death in 1912.

Gertrud Eysoldt (1870–1950). A Reinhardt actress much

praised for her fascinating interpretations of Strindberg and Wedekind roles; she was a celebrated Lulu.

Tilly Newes (1886-1970). An Austrian actress who attracted attention as Leontine in Hauptmann's *The Beaver Coat*. Wedekind promoted her career and married her in 1906. She became a famous exponent of his major female roles and often played them opposite him.

Ida Orloff (1889-1945). A Brahm discovery. Played Lulu, and Klara in Wedekind's *Music*. Hauptmann was captivated by her portrayal of Hannele and created his Pippa for her in 1906 when she was sixteen. Her affair with Hauptmann was short-lived. She moved from Berlin to Vienna in 1910. By then her brief career as an enchantingly popular actress was almost over.

Paula Wessely (born 1907). Vienna-based actress. A fine Christine in Schnitzler's *Liebelei* (in 1933) and Genia Hofreiter in *The Vast Domain* (in 1959). She was also a noted Wendla in Wedekind's *Spring Awakening* and Rose Bernd in Hauptmann's play.

Emanuel Reicher (1849-1924). Germany's first great Naturalist actor. Closely associated with the breakthrough of Ibsen in Germany, he became a mainstay of Brahm's ensemble. A fine Ibsen actor, he created Johannes Vockerat in Hauptmann's *Lonely Lives*, and produced *The Weavers* in English (New York, 1915).

Oscar Sauer (1856-1918). A leading member of Brahm's ensemble, with a particular gift of bringing out character and making even minor roles interesting. A noted Wehrhahn in Hauptmann's *The Beaver Coat*, he suffered from spinal paralysis, which later in his career forced him to act in a sitting position.

Josef Kainz (1858–1910). Famous actor associated with the Deutsches Theater in Berlin until 1899, when he moved to the Vienna Burgtheater to become the most highly regarded German classical actor of his day. Though less happy in contemporary drama, he created Wilhelm Scholz in *The Reconciliation*, Bäcker in *The Weavers* and Heinrich in *The Sunken Bell*. He also played the title role in Schnitzler's *Paracelsus* and had hoped to create those of Hofreiter in Schnitzler's *The Vast Domain* and the Marquis von Keith in Wedekind's play. Hauptmann echoed the general opinion when he called him 'a prince among actors'.

Albert Bassermann (1867–1952). Joined Brahm's ensemble in 1900 but went over to Reinhardt in 1909. Especially successful in Ibsen, he was also a notable Crampton in Hauptmann's comedy *Colleague Crampton*, and created the part of Sala in Schnitzler's *The Lonely Way* (Berlin, 1904). After the death of Kainz in 1910 he was widely regarded as the leading German actor. He starred in Leopold Jessner's *Erdgeist* film of 1923 opposite Asta Nielsen. He later emigrated to the United States, but returned to Germany after the war.

Rudolf Rittner (1869–1943). Actor closely associated with Brahm's ensemble at the Deutsches Theater, and with the Lessing-Theater in Berlin. Germany's leading Naturalist actor, he created and played many important Hauptmann roles (Florian Geyer, Henschel, Flamm, and the forest goblin in *The Sunken Bell*). He gave up acting in 1907 at the height of his powers to take up farming in Silesia.

Werner Krauss (1884–1959). Often played under Reinhardt

in Berlin. A noted Schigolch in Wedekind's Lulu plays, he also created the part of Clausen in Hauptmann's *Before Sunset*, playing it in London in 1933 in Miles Malleson's English adaptation.

The Theatres

Berlin

Deutsches Theater (opened 1883). Set up by a group of actors in 1883 with a view to performing the classics free from conventional melodramatic pathos. Owned and managed by the popular playwright Adolph L'Arronge, its policy stressed careful casting and production, rehearsal and ensemble work. Under Otto Brahm (1894–1904) it became the home of German Naturalism. In 1905 it was taken over by Max Reinhardt.

Lessing-Theater (opened 1888). Managed by Oscar Blumenthal, it concentrated on contemporary problem-plays, opening with Ibsen's *A Doll's House*. Blumenthal was quick to see the financial advantages of the new Naturalism (especially Sudermann and Duse), and provided space for the Freie Bühne. From 1904 to 1912, under Otto Brahm, it became *the* Naturalist house. It was taken over by Viktor Barnowsky in 1913.

Residenz-Theater (founded 1871). Specialised in light entertainment and social comedy in the French manner and excelled in the conversational style. It later backed Ibsen and Strindberg.

Kleines Theater. From 1902 run by Max Reinhardt and from 1905 by Barnowsky. The first Berlin production of Wedekind's *Earth Spirit* took place there in 1902.

Kammerspiele. A small experimental theatre (1906) associated with Reinhardt. The première of Wedekind's *Spring Awakening* was given there in 1906.

Neues Theater. Another Reinhardt house which played Wedekind.

Freie Bühne (Berlin Free Stage Society). Set up in April 1889, it was modelled on André Antoine's experimental Théâtre Libre (1887) in Paris. Its first season consisted of ten Sunday matinées in the Lessing-Theater; it then moved to the Residenz-Theater. Its stage activities were sporadic after 1891.

Vienna

Burgtheater (Imperial Court Theatre). Was and still is the principal theatre in Vienna. Founded in 1776, it moved to its new location in the Ringstrasse in 1888. Under Max Burckhard (1890–8) it broadened its repertoire to include modern drama (Ibsen, Hauptmann and Schnitzler), but Burckhard's pioneering zeal led to conflict with the authorities and to his resignation. He was succeeded by Paul Schlenther (1898–1910). Thirteen Schnitzler plays were premièred at the Burgtheater between 1895 and 1931.

Theater in der Josefstadt. From 1899 this venerable theatre promoted modern drama and was later associated with Max Reinhardt and Schnitzler's producer son Heinrich Schnitzler. It played Wedekind and was an early promoter of Schnitzler's *Anatol*.

Deutsches Volkstheater. Opened in 1889. Its policy was to provide high-quality, middle-of-the-road entertainment. Its repertoire embraced classical and modern plays.

Munich

Schauspielhaus. Under the direction of Georg Stolberg this theatre was closely associated with Wedekind as actor, producer and literary adviser. The first 'Wedekind season', with the playwright and Tilly Newes in all the leading roles, was put on there in 1906.

Künstlertheater. Opened in 1908 and aimed to renew the German theatre by rejecting the Naturalist tradition. Plays were to be presented as such; the auditorium was an amphitheatre facing a shallow stage on which the action could be presented like a stylised fresco or bas-relief.

Select Bibliography

Critical Works in English

HAUPTMANN

H. F. Garten, *Gerhart Hauptmann* (Cambridge: Bowes and Bowes, and New Haven: Yale University Press, both 1954); and 'Gerhart Hauptmann', in *German Men of Letters*, ed. Alex Natan (London: Wolff, 1961) pp. 235-49.

Margaret Sinden, *Gerhart Hauptmann: The Prose Plays* (Toronto: University of Toronto Press, 1957): remains the best academic study of Hauptmann's drama in English.

WEDEKIND

Alan Best, *Frank Wedekind* (London: Wolff, 1975).

Elizabeth Boa, *The Sexual Circus: Wedekind's Theatre of Subversion* (Oxford: Basil Blackwell, 1987).

Sol Gittleman, *Wedekind*, Twayne's World Author Series no. 55 (New York: Twayne, 1969).

Alex Natan, 'Frank Wedekind', in *German Men of Letters II*, ed. Natan (London: Wolff, 1963) pp. 103-29.

163

SCHNITZLER

H. B. Garland, 'Arthur Schnitzler', in *German Men of Letters II*, ed. Alex Natan (London: Wolff, 1963) pp. 57–75.

Martin Swales, *Arthur Schnitzler: A Critical Study* (Oxford: Clarendon Press, 1971).

Reinhard Urbach, *Arthur Schnitzler* (New York: Ungar, 1973). See too the informative articles by Stephanie Hammer and Gerd Schneider on the American stage-history of *Anatol*, *Liebelei* and *The Round Dance* in *Modern Austrian Literature*, 19 (1986).

GENERAL

Horst Claus, *The Theater Director Otto Brahm* (Ann Arbor: University of Michigan Press, 1981).

John Osborne, *The Naturalist Drama in Germany* (Manchester: Manchester University Press, 1971).

Leroy R. Shaw, *The Playwright and Historical Change: Dramatic Strategies in Brecht, Hauptmann, Kaiser and Wedekind* (Madison: University of Wisconsin Press, 1970).

Critical Works in German

HAUPTMANN

Roy C. Cowen, *Hauptmann-Kommentar zum dramatischen Werk* (Munich: Winkler, 1980): a detailed study of the sources, composition and critical reception of each play.

Karl S. Guthke, *Gerhart Hauptmann: Weltbild im Werk* (Göttingen, 1961; 2nd, rev. edn Berne: Francke, 1980): a major study of the writer's evolving world view.

F. W. J. Heuser, *Gerhart Hauptmann. Zu seinem Leben und Schaffen* (Tübingen: Niemeyer, 1961): a collection of reminiscences and essays containing an account of Hauptmann's relationship with Wedekind.

Eberhard Hilscher, *Gerhart Hauptmann* (Berlin: Verlag der

Nation, 1969): still the authoritative critical biography.

Sigfrid Hoefert, *Gerhart Hauptmann*, Sammlung Metzler 107 (Stuttgart: Metzler, 1974; 2nd, rev. edn 1982): an essential bibliographical handbook.

——, *Internationale Bibliographie zum Werk Gerhart Hauptmanns*, vol. I (Berlin: Erich Schmidt, 1986): lists all the English and American translations and editions of Hauptmann's works.

Rolf Michaelis, *Der schwarze Zeus: Gerhart Hauptmanns zweiter Weg* (Berlin: Argon Verlag, 1962): a sensitive exploration of the 'other' Hauptmann and his less well-known dramas.

Peter Sprengel, *Gerhart Hauptmann: Epoche – Werk – Wirkung* (Munich: Beck, 1984): a well-informed account of many of the major works.

K. L. Tank, *Gerhart Hauptmann in Selbstzeugnissen und Bilddokumenten* (Reinbek: Rowohlt, 1959): an illustrated paperback biographical study.

H. D. Tschörtner, *Ungeheures erhofft: Zu Gerhart Hauptmann – Werk und Wirkung* (Berlin: Buchverlag Der Morgen, 1986): a GDR publication which brings together interesting essays on the relationship of Hauptmann to Brecht and James Joyce.

WEDEKIND

H.-J. Irmer, *Der Theaterdichter Frank Wedekind* (Berlin: Henschelverlag, 1975; 2nd edn 1979): the major general survey of the dramatist's work.

Arthur Kutscher, *Wedekind, Leben und Werk* (Munich: List, 1964): 2nd, rev. edn of the standard critical biography of 1922–31.

Günter Seehaus, *Frank Wedekind und das Theater* (Munich: Laocoon Verlag, 1964): authoritative German stage-history of Wedekind's plays.

——, *Frank Wedekind mit Selbstzeugnissen und Bilddokumenten* (Reinbek: Rowohlt, 1974): an illustrated paperback biographical survey.

Hartmut Vinçon, *Frank Wedekind*, Sammlung Metzler 230 (Stuttgart: Metzler, 1986): the first comprehensive bibliographical guide to the life and works.

SCHNITZLER

H.-U. Lindken, *Arthur Schnitzler: Aspekte und Akzente— Materialien zu Leben und Werk* (Berne: Lang, 1984): an important collection of material concerning Schnitzler's life and works.

Michaela L. Perlmann, *Arthur Schnitzler*, Sammlung Metzler 239 (Stuttgart: Metzler, 1987): the first comprehensive bibliographical guide to the life and works.

Heinz Rieder, *Arthur Schnitzler: Das dichterische Werk* (Vienna: Bergland, 1973).

Hartmut Scheible, *Arthur Schnitzler in Selbstzeugnissen und Bilddokumenten* (Reinbek: Rowohlt, 1976): an illustrated paperback biographical survey.

Heinrich Schnitzler, Christian Brandstätter and Reinhard Unger, *Arthur Schnitzler: Sein Leben, sein Werk, seine Zeit* (Frankfurt-am-Main: Fischer, 1981): an illustrated account of the writer's life and times.

Reinhard Urbach, *Schnitzler-Kommentar zu den erzählenden Schriften und dramatischen Werken* (Munich: Winkler, 1974): a commentary on the genesis and reception of the individual works.

Renate Wagner, *Arthur Schnitzler* (Frankfurt-am-Main: Fischer, 1984): the up-to-date biography.

Renate Wagner and Brigitte Vacha, *Wiener Schnitzler-Aufführungen 1891-1970* (Munich: Prestel, 1971): a Viennese stage history of Schnitzler's plays.

Select Bibliography

GENERAL

H.-P. Bayerdörfer, K. O. Conrady, H. Schanze (eds), *Literatur und Theater im Wilhelminischen Zeitalter* (Tübingen, Niemeyer, 1978): a collection of wide-ranging essays on the stage in Germany between 1871 and 1914.

Norbert Jaron, Renate Möhrmann, Hedwig Müller, *Berlin-Theater der Jahrhundertwende* (Tübingen: Niemeyer, 1978): a stage-history of Berlin between 1889 and 1914 as reflected in contemporary play reviews.

Gernot Schley, *Die Freie Bühne in Berlin* (Berlin: Haude und Spener, 1967).

Index

Index